Workbook

WORLD ENGLISH Intro

SECOND EDITION

Real People • Real Places • Real Language

Kristin L. Johannsen, Author
Rob Jenkins, Series Editor

T0306513

NATIONAL GEOGRAPHIC LEARNING | CENGAGE Learning

Australia • Brazil • Japan • Korea • Mexico • Singapore • Spain • United Kingdom • United States

NATIONAL GEOGRAPHIC LEARNING | CENGAGE Learning

World English Intro Workbook
Real People, Real Places, Real Language
Kristin L. Johannsen, Author
Rob Jenkins, Series Editor

Publisher: Sherrise Roehr
Executive Editor: Sarah Kenney
Senior Development Editor: Margarita Matte
Development Editor: Brenden Layte
Assistant Editor: Alison Bruno
Editorial Assistant: Patricia Giunta
Media Researcher: Leila Hishmeh
Senior Technology Product Manager: Scott Rule
Director of Global Marketing: Ian Martin
Senior Product Marketing Manager: Caitlin Thomas
Senior Director of ELT Production: Michael Burggren
Production Manager: Daisy Sosa
Content Project Manager: Andrea Bobotas
Senior Print Buyer: Mary Beth Hennebury
Cover Designer: Aaron Opie
Art Director: Scott Baker
Creative Director: Chris Roy
Cover Image: Martin Roemers/Panos Pictures
Compositor: MPS Limited

World English Intro Workbook ISBN: 978-1-285-84842-6

National Geographic Learning
20 Channel Center Street
Boston, MA 02210
USA

Cengage Learning is a leading provider of customized learning solutions with office locations around the globe, including Singapore, the United Kingdom, Austrailia, Mexico, Brazil, and Japan.

Cengage Learning products are represented in Canada by Nelson Education, Ltd.

Visit National Geographic Learning online at ngl.cengage.com

Visit our corporate website at www.cengage.com

Printed in the United States of America
6 7 8 9 10 22 21 20 19

CONTENTS

STUDENT BOOK SCOPE AND SEQUENCE

	Unit Goals	Grammar	Vocabulary
UNIT 1 **Friends and Family** Page 2 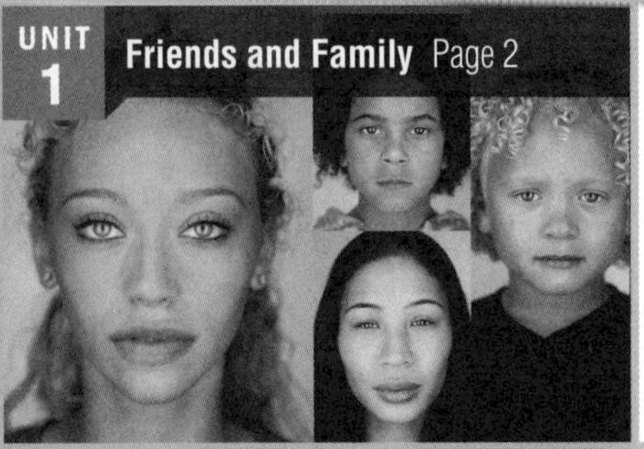	• Meet and introduce people • Identify family members • Describe people • Present your family	Present tense *be* *I'**m** Kim.* *They'**re** Maria and Lola.* *Be* + adjective *They'**re young. Is** John **single**?* Questions with *be* and short answers ***Are** you married? Yes, I **am**/ No I'**m not.***	Greetings and introductions Family members Adjectives to describe people
UNIT 2 **Jobs Around the World** Page 14 	• Identify jobs • Talk about jobs • Talk about countries • Compare jobs in different countries	Contractions with *be:* Negative; Indefinite articles *He **isn't** a doctor. Pat's **an** artist.* *Be* + article + adjective + noun *Russia **is a big country.***	Jobs Numbers Words to describe the weather Continents, countries, and cities
UNIT 3 **Houses and Apartments** Page 26 	• Identify places in a home • Describe your house • Identify household objects • Compare houses	*There is/there are* ***There are** three bedrooms.* ***Is there** a garage?* Prepositions of place: *in, on, under, next to* *Your magazine is **under** your bag.*	Places in a home Furniture and household objects
TEDTALKS **Video** Page 38 **Kent Larson: Brilliant Designs to Fit More People in Every City** Video Strategy: Using Visual Cues			
UNIT 4 **Possessions** Page 42 	• Identify personal possessions • Talk about other people's possessions • Buy a present • Talk about special possessions	Demonstrative adjectives *Are **these** your books? **That** is not your bag.* Possessive nouns *It's **Jim's** bag.* *Have* *She **has** a camcorder.*	Personal possessions Electronic products
UNIT 5 **Daily Activities** Page 54 	• Tell time • Talk about people's daily activities • Talk about what you do at work or school • Describe a job	Simple present tense: statements, negatives, *What time...?* questions, and short answers *They **get up** at 7 o'clock. What time **do** you **start** work?* Adverbs of frequency: *always, sometimes, never* *I **never** answer the phone.* Time expressions	Daily activities Telling time Work and school activities Time expressions
UNIT 6 **Getting There** Page 66 	• Ask for and give directions • Create and use a tour route • Describe transportation • Record a journey	Prepositions of Place; Imperatives ***Turn** left and **walk** for two blocks. The hotel is **across from** the park.* *Have to* *She **has to** change buses.*	City landmarks Directions Ground transportation
TEDTALKS **Video** Page 78 **Karen Bass: Unseen Footage, Untamed Nature**			

Listening	Speaking and Pronunciation	Reading	Writing	Video Journal
Listening for general understanding and specific information People describing their families	Talking about your family The /*r*/ sound	**National Geographic:** "Families around the World"	Writing sentences to describe your family	**National Geographic:** "Animal Families"
Focused listening People describing their jobs	Asking for and giving personal information Numbers Contractions with *be*	**National Geographic:** "Different Farmers"	Writing a paragraph to describe a person's job	**National Geographic:** "A Job for Children"
Listening for general understanding and specific details People talking about their houses	Describing your house Final *–s*	**TED**TALKS "Kent Larson: Brilliant Designs to Fit More People in Every City"	Writing descriptions of houses Writing Strategy: Topic Sentence	**National Geographic:** "A Very Special Village"
Listening for specific information People proving ownership	Talking about the personal possessions of others /iː/ and /ɪ/ sounds	**National Geographic:** "Jewelry"	Summarizing a class survey Using commas	**National Geographic:** "Uncovering the Past"
Listening for general understanding and specific details Describing a photographer's work	Asking and answering questions about work or school activities Falling intonation on statements and information questions	**TED**TALKS "Karen Bass: Unseen Footage, Untamed Nature"	Writing a job description	**National Geographic:** "Zoo Dentists"
Listening for specific information Radio ad for a tour	Ask for and give directions *Yes/no* questions and short answers	**National Geographic:** "Journey to Antarctica"	Writing a travel itinerary	**National Geographic:** "Volcano Trek"

	Unit Goals	Grammar	Vocabulary
UNIT 7 **Free Time** Page 82 	• Identify activities that are happening now • Make a phone call • Talk about abilities • Talk about sports	Present continuous tense ***I'm not watching** TV. **I'm reading.*** *Can* (for ability) *He **can't** play the guitar. He **can** sing.*	Pastimes Games and sports
UNIT 8 **Clothes** Page 94 	• Identify and shop for clothes • Buy clothes • Express likes and dislikes • Learn about clothes and colors	*Can/could* (for polite requests) ***Can** I try on these shoes?* Likes and dislikes *I **love** your sweater! She **hates** pink.*	Colors Clothes
UNIT 9 **Eat Well** Page 106 	• Order a meal • Plan a party • Describe your diet • Talk about a healthy diet	*Some, any* *There's **some** ice cream in the fridge.* *How much/how many* ***How many** oranges do we need? **How much** chocolate do we have?*	Food types Meals Quantities Count/non-count nouns
TEDTALKS **Video** Page 118 **Ron Finley: A Guerilla Gardener in South Central L.A.** Video Strategy: Using Visual Cues			
UNIT 10 **Health** Page 122 	• Identify parts of the body to say how you feel • Ask about and describe symptoms • Identify remedies and give advice • Describe how to prevent health problems	Review of simple present tense My back ***hurts***. *Look* + adjective *Feel* + adjective John ***looks*** terrible. I ***feel*** sick. *Should* (for advice) *You **should** take an aspirin.*	Parts of the body Common illnesses Remedies
UNIT 11 **Making Plans** Page 134 	• Plan special days • Describe holiday traditions • Make life plans • Express wishes and plans	*Be going to* *What **are** you **going to** do? We **are going to** have a party.* *Would like to* (for wishes) *I **would like to** be a doctor.*	Special plans American holidays Professions
UNIT 12 **On the Move** Page 146 	• Use the simple past • Give biographical information • Describe a move • Discuss migrations	Simple past tense *We **went** to the mountains. He **moved** from San Francisco to New York.*	Verbs + prepositions of movement Preparing to move
TEDTALKS **Video** Page 158 **Derek Sivers: Weird or Different?**			

Listening	Speaking and Pronunciation	Reading	Writing	Video Journal
Listening for specific information Telephone conversation	Have a phone conversation /ʃ/ and /tʃ/ sounds *Can* and *can't*	**National Geographic:** "Soccer—The Beautiful Game"	Writing sentences about your abilities	**National Geographic:** "Danny's Challenge"
Listening for specific details Listening to people shopping for clothes	Describing people's clothes *Could you*	**National Geographic:** "Chameleon Clothes"	Writing about what people are wearing	**National Geographic:** "Traditional Silk-Making"
Listening for specific details Conversation to confirm a shopping list	Planning a dinner *And*	**TED**TALKS "Ron Finley: A Guerilla Gardener in South Central L.A."	Writing sentences about eating habits Writing Strategy: Self-Correct	**National Geographic:** "Slow Food"
Listening for general understanding and specific details Describing symptoms to a doctor	Describing symptoms and illnesses; giving advice Sentence stress	**National Geographic:** "Preventing Disease"	Writing a paragraph on disease prevention	**National Geographic:** "Farley, the Red Panda"
Listening for general understanding and specific details American holiday traditions	Talking about celebrating holidays *Be going to* (reduced form)	**TED**TALKS "Derek Sivers: Keep Your Goals to Yourself"	Writing about one's plans for the future	**National Geographic:** "Making a Thai Boxing Champion"
Listening for general understanding and specific details Biographies of famous immigrants	Discussing moving *–ed* endings	**National Geographic:** "Human Migration"	Writing a vacation postcard	**National Geographic:** "Monarch Migration"

CREDITS

PHOTO

Cover Photo: Martin Roemers/Panos Pictures

10: (1) © iStockphoto.com/YinYang, (2) © iStockphoto.com/digitalskillet, (3) © iStockphoto.com/digitalskillet, (4) © iStockphoto.com/mamahoohooba, (5 left) © iStockphoto.com/bo1982, (5 right) © iStockphoto.com/bbossom, (6) © iStockphoto.com/stevecoleimages, (7) © Apollofoto/Shutterstock.com; **11:** (1) © iStockphoto.com/arekmalang, (2) Image Source/Getty Images, (3) © iStockphoto.com/MBI_Images, (4) © iStockphoto.com/graffoto8, (5) © T-Design/Shutterstock.com, (6) Image Source/Getty Images, (7) Miroslav Ferkuniak/Dreamstime.com, (8) © iStockphoto.com/theboone; **12:** (bottom) © iStockphoto.com/TAGSTOCK1; **15:** (1) © iStockphoto.com/NadejdaReid, (2) © Diego Cervo/Shutterstock.com, (3) © Francis Wong Chee Yen/Shutterstock.com, (4) © iStockphoto.com/YinYang, (5) © iStockphoto.com/njgphoto, (6) © AVAVA/Shutterstock.com, (7) © iStockphoto.com/KentWeakley, (8) © iStockphoto.com/RobertDupuis; **21:** (1) © Rodenberg Photography/Shutterstock.com, (2) Irina88w/Dreamstime.com, (3) © Baloncici/Shutterstock.com, (4) © iStockphoto.com/Pinopic, (5) Thomas Barwick/Getty Images, (6) Maxym022/Dreamstime.com, (7) © iStockphoto.com/gerenme, (8) © pics721/Shutterstock.com; **22:** (middle) © iStockphoto.com/adpower99, (bottom) © iStockphoto.com/Yvan Dubé; **28:** (top) Hans Surfer/Moment/Getty Images; **29:** (1) Gae13/Dreamstime.com, (2) © iStockphoto.com/Stephen Krow, (3) © iStockphoto.com/kodobist, (4) © iStockphoto.com/hudiemm, (5) Digifoto Diamond/Alamy, (6) © iStockphoto.com/CostinT, (7) © Milos Luzanin/Shutterstock.com, (8) 55hasan/Dreamstime.com; **30:** (top right) © iStockphoto.com/Becart, (middle left) © iStockphoto.com/RonTech2000, (bottom right) © iStockphoto.com/umahtete; **31:** © iStockphoto.com/JJRD; **33:** (1) © StockLite/Shutterstock.com, (2) © iStockphoto.com/killerb10, (3) © iStockphoto.com/InspiredFootage, (4) © iStockphoto.com/Neustockimages, (5) Joel Sartore/National Geographic Creative, (6) © iStockphoto.com/Oktay Ortakcioglu; **34:** (top) © iStockphoto.com/mgkaya, (middle) Hongqi Zhang/Alamy; **36:** (top) altrendo images/Getty Images, (middle) © iStockphoto.com/KateLeigh, (bottom) © Monika Wisniewska/Shutterstock.com; **37:** © Rob Marmion/Shutterstock.com; **39:** (1) © iStockphoto.com/monkeybusinessimages; (2) © iStockphoto.com/MorePixels; (3) © iStockphoto.com/Justin Horrocks, (4) © iStockphoto.com/3bugsmom, (5) © iStockphoto.com/Juanmonino, (6) © iStockphoto.com/Brian Raisbeck, (7) © iStockphoto.com/Gesundheit, (8) © ExaMedia Photography/Shutterstock.com, (9) mediacolor's/Alamy, (10) Michael Coyne/Getty Images, (11) Michael Dwyer/Alamy, (12) David R. Frazier Photolibrary, Inc/Alamy; **40:** (left) View Stock/Alamy; **41:** (1) © iStockphoto.com/Rakdee, (2) © iStockphoto.com/Rakdee, (3) © iStockphoto.com/Rakdee, (4) © iStockphoto.com/Rakdee; **42:** (top) P. Batchelder/Alamy; **43:** (top) © iStockphoto.com/shaunl, (middle) © iStockphoto.com/Dirk Freder, (bottom left) © iStockphoto.com/guysargent, (bottom right) © iStockphoto.com/Veni; **46:** (top) © iStockphoto.com/Lise Gagne, (bottom) © iStockphoto.com/OJO_Images; **47:** (1) © iStockphoto.com/microgen, (2) © iStockphoto.com/Sportstock, (3) © iStockphoto.com/ YinYang, (4) © iStockphoto.com/Matt_Brown, (5) © iStockphoto.com/technotr, (6) © iStockphoto.com/Leonardo Patrizi, (7) Erwin Purnomo Sidi/Dreamstime.com. (8) © iStockphoto.com/kelvinjay; **48:** (c) AP Images/Francois Mori; **49:** (top) xPACIFICA/National Geographic Creative, (top middle) © iStockphoto.com/Syldavia, (bottom middle) © iStockphoto.com/gbh007, (bottom), ©Tatiana Popova/Shutterstock.com; **52:** (top) © iStockphoto.com/FotoSpeedy; **53:** (1) © iStockphoto.com/pixitive, (2) © iStockphoto.com/magnetcreative, (3) Bjørn Hovdal/Dreamstime.com, (4) © iStockphoto.com/Floortje, (5) © iStockphoto.com/Muhla1, (6) © iStockphoto.com/Entienou, (7) © iStockphoto.com/bluekite, (8) © iStockphoto.com/konradlew; **55:** (top) © iStockphoto.com/JustinVoight, (bottom) © iStockphoto.com/GlobalStock; **58:** Eri Morita/The Image Bank/Getty Images; **60:** (left) © Peter Baxter/Shutterstock.com, (middle) © wizdata1/Shutterstock.com, (right) James Roman/iStock 360/Getty Images; **61:** (left) © iStockphoto.com/vgajic, (middle) © iStockphoto.com/smpics, (right) Stock Connection/SuperStock; **64:** (1) © Carlos Caetano/Shutterstock.com, (2) © iStockphoto.com/WillSelarep, (3) © iStockphoto.com/digitalskillet, (4) © iStockphoto.com/Yuri_Arcurs, (5) © Adam Gregor/Shutterstock.com; **65:** (top) © Rob Marmion/Shutterstock.com, (bottom) © iStockphoto.com/dardespot; **66:** (top) © iStockphoto.com/Kirby Hamilton, (bottom) © iStockphoto.com/Bogdan Kosanovic; **67:** (bottom) © joannawnuk/Shutterstock.com; **69:** (1) ©istockphoto.com/Shelly Perry, (2) Blend Images/Alamy, (3) © iStockphoto.com/webphotographeer, (4) © iStockphoto.com/SolStock, (5) © wavebreakmedia/Shutterstock.com, (6) © Celso Pupo/Shutterstock.com; **70:** (top) Christophe Boisvieux/Age Fototstock, (middle) © iStockphoto.com/Vitalina Rybakova, (bottom) Stanislav Sokolov/Age Fotostock; **71:** right Fotosearch/Getty Images; **72:** right © iStockphoto.com/pafe, (left top) © iStockphoto.com/furtaev, (left middle) © Sheftsoff/Shuterstock.com, (left bottom) © istockphoto.com/Neustockimages; **75:** (top) © iStockphoto.com/mamahoohooba, (bottom) © iStockphoto.com/Vikram Raghuvanshi; **77:** (1) Image Source/Getty Images, (2) © V. J. Matthew/Shutterstock.com, (3) © iStockphoto.com/asasirov, (4) © StockLite/Shutterstock.com, (5) © iStockphoto.com/YinYang, (6) Image Source/Digital Vision/Getty Images, (7) © iStockphoto.com/Squaredpixels, (8) © Blinka/Shutterstock.com; **79:** (top right) © luca amedei/Shutterstock.com, (bottom left) © iStockphoto.com/uschools, (bottom right) © iStockphoto.com/zarinmedia.

ILLUSTRATION:

9: Keith Neely/Illustration Online.com; **12:** Keith Neely/IllustrationOnline.com; **16:** Ted Hammond/IllustrationOnline.com; **18–19:** Ralph Voltz/IllustrationOnline.com; **23:** Patrick Gnan/IllustrationOnline.com; **24:** Ralph Voltz/IllustrationOnline.com; **27:** Ted Hammond/IllustrationOnline.com; **28:** Ralph Voltz/IllustrationOnline.com; **40–41:** (5) Kenneth Batelman; **42:** (1) (2) (5) (6) Ted Hammond/IllustrationOnline.com; **42:** (3) (4) Patrick Gnan/IllustrationOnline.com; **45:** Ralph Voltz/IllustrationOnline.com; **51:** Ted Hammond/IllustrationOnline.com; **54:** Nesbitt Graphics (all insets are Ted Hammond/IllustrationOnline.com); **57:** Patrick Gnan/IllustrationOnline.com; **59:** Patrick Gnan/IllustrationOnline.com; **63:** Ralph Voltz/IllustrationOnline.com; **73:** National Geographic Maps; **76:** Ralph Voltz/IllustrationOnline.com; **78:** National Geographic Maps.

FRIENDS AND FAMILY

Lesson A GRAMMAR AND VOCABULARY

A Unscramble the conversations. Add capitals and punctuation.

1. **A:** it hi how's going Hi. How's it going?
   B: fine you and ______
2. **A:** good how you morning are ______
   B: fine how thank and are you you ______
3. **A:** this friend is Yong-Jun my ______
   B: you nice meet to Yong-Jun ______
   C: nice too to meet you ______

B Write the sentences again. Use contractions.

1. We are Tom and Jason. We're Tom and Jason.
2. He is Mr. Smith. ______
3. I am Aisha. ______
4. You are Stefan. ______
5. They are Luis and Marta. ______
6. She is Noriko. ______

C Complete the sentences with possessive adjectives (*my, your, his, her, their, our*).

1. His name is Jacob.

2. ______ name is Jenny.

3. ______ names are Jenny and Katelyn.

4. ______ names are Mr. and Mrs. Lee.

5. ______ name is Annie.

6. ______ name is Mr. Black.

Lesson B GRAMMAR AND VOCABULARY

A Unscramble the family members.

1. refaht _father_
2. therom ______
3. rotherb ______
4. retiss ______
5. fagraertndh ______
6. ranthomderg ______
7. andbush ______
8. hdilrcne ______
9. ranspte ______
10. sngteradpran ______

B Label the people in the family tree.

1. _grandfather_ 2. ______

3. ______ 4. ______

5. ______ _me_ 6. ______

7. ______

C Complete each sentence with a word from the box.

are	his	is	their	her

1. These are my grandparents. ______ names are Takumi and Miku.
2. These ______ my parents. Their names are Kaito and Miyu.
3. This is my sister. ______ name is Keiko.
4. This is my husband. ______ name is Yamato.
5. This ______ our son. His name is Daito.

Lesson C GRAMMAR AND VOCABULARY

married	tall	short	young
handsome	old	single	pretty

A Label the pictures with words from the box.

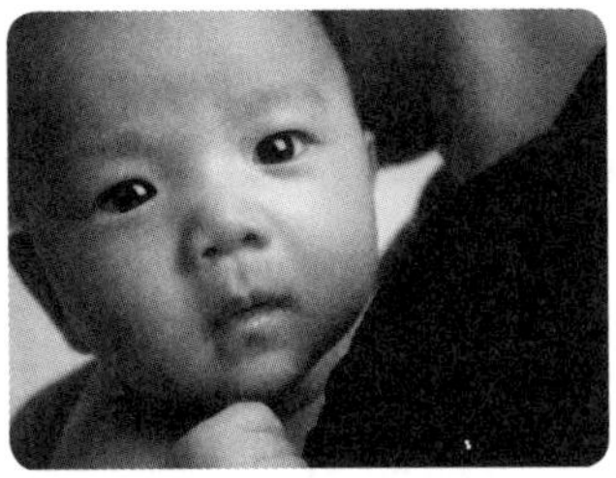

1. ________________

2. ________________

3. ________________

4. ________________

5. ________________

6. ________________

7. ________________

8. ________________

B Describe people in your family.

1. My grandmother is short with curly gray hair.
2. My father is ________________ with ________________.
3. My ________________________________.
4. ________________________________.
5. ________________________________.

C Complete the conversations.

1. **A:** You're tall and blond. __________ your sister tall, too?
   B: No, __________. She's __________ and has curly black hair.

2. **A:** __________ your brothers married?
   B: David __________ married. His wife __________ very attractive. Paul __________ married. __________ single.

D Answer the questions.

1. Are you tall? ________________________
2. Are you married? ________________________
3. Are your parents old? ________________________
4. Is your hair curly? ________________________

Two Families

A Read about the two families.

This is the Carter family. Nancy and Jeff are married. Nancy is short with long blond hair. Her husband Jeff is tall with wavy black hair. They have three children, a son and two daughters. Their son is David. He is tall with short, curly brown hair. Their daughters are Sara and Emma. They are pretty. They both have long straight hair like their mother.

Meet Hiroshi Yamada and his family. Hiroshi is tall and handsome with short black hair. His wife is Mari. Mari is pretty with long, straight black hair. They have two children, a son and a daughter. Their son is Yuji. He has very short hair. Their daughter is Aya. She is pretty with long hair. They both have straight black hair like their parents.

B Write the name.

1. Hiroshi is her husband. ____________________
2. Nancy is his wife. ____________________
3. Aya is his sister. ____________________
4. David is their brother. ____________________ and ____________________
5. Yuji and Aya are his children. ____________________
6. Mari is their mother. ____________________ and ____________________
7. Jeff is their father. __________, __________, and __________
8. Sara is her sister. ____________________

C Circle *Yes* or *No.*

1. David has two sisters.	Yes	No
2. Hiroshi is short.	Yes	No
3. Jeff has straight hair.	Yes	No
4. Nancy has three children.	Yes	No
5. Mari is single.	Yes	No
6. Sara and Emma are twins.	Yes	No
7. Yuji has curly hair.	Yes	No
8. Mari is pretty.	Yes	No

D Draw a picture of your family. Write sentences about the people.

1. My grandfather is old. He is tall with short, wavy gray hair.
2. ____________________
3. ____________________
4. ____________________

Review

A Solve the crossword puzzle with vocabulary and grammar from this unit.

Across

1. _______ name is Young-Mi. I'm from Korea.
4. This is my mother. _______ name is Mary.
5. _______ your brother married?
7. My _______ is very old. He's 92 years old!
11. This is my father. _______ name is Mark.
12. Annie is _______. She's 7 years old.

Down

1. Paulo is _______. Alina is his wife.
2. I have one sister and two _______.
3. These are my friends. _______ names are Mia and Alex.
6. "Are you married?" "No, I'm _______."
7. _______ afternoon!
8. How _______ you?
9. My father, mother, sisters, and brother are my _______.
10. Hi! _______ it going?

B Complete the description with words from the box.

sister	daughter	tall
long	married	~~name~~
wavy	children	

My (1) ___name___ is Samuel. I'm (2) ________________ with (3) ________________, straight brown hair. I have one (4) ________________. She is Isabel. She is young with long (5) ________________ hair. I'm (6) ________________.
My wife is Natalia. She is short with curly blond hair. We have two (7) ________________, a son and a (8) ________________.

C Write a description of you and your family. Use words from the unit.

____

____

____

____

____

JOBS AROUND THE WORLD

Lesson A GRAMMAR AND VOCABULARY

A Write a sentence about these jobs.

1. He's a taxi driver.

2. ____________

3. ____________

4. ____________

5. ____________

6. ____________

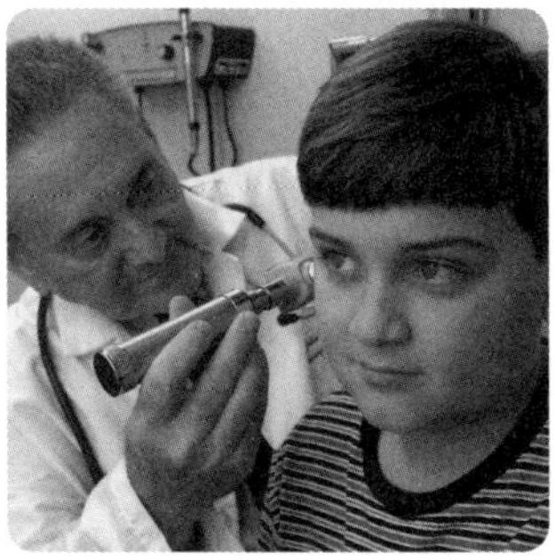

7. ____________

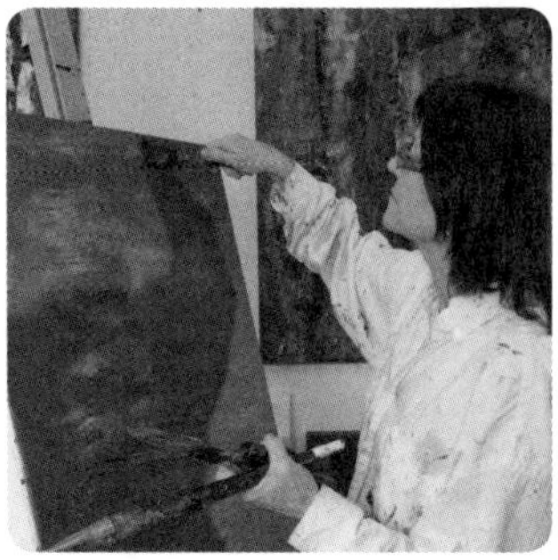

8. ____________

B Write negative sentences. Use contractions.

1. He's a student. He isn't a student.
2. They're old. ____________
3. She's an architect. ____________
4. You're a teacher. ____________
5. We're tall. ____________
6. It's interesting. ____________

C Write the correct indefinite article: *a* or *an.*

1. a teacher	3. ____ daughter	5. ____ job	7. ____ engineer	9. ____ chef
2. ____ architect	4. ____ child	6. ____ son	8. ____ husband	10. ____ artist

D Write the answers for the questions.

He's 23. ~~She's fine~~. They're good. Yes, he is.

1. **A:** How's your wife?
   B: She's fine.
2. **A:** How are the children?
   B: ____________
3. **A:** How old is Steven now?
   B: ____________
4. **A:** Is he married?
   B: ____________

Lesson B GRAMMAR AND VOCABULARY

A Unscramble the questions. Write your answers.

1. (what your is name) What is your name ______?
   My name is ______.
2. (are how you old) ______?
   ______.
3. (job is what your) ______?
   ______.
4. (your is job interesting) ______?
   ______.
5. (old is father how your) ______?
   ______.
6. (job what his is) ______?
   ______.
7. (job interesting is his) ______?
   ______.

B Read the answers. Write the questions.

1. What is your name ______?
   My name is Mayumi Tanaka.
2. ______?
   I'm 29 years old.
3. ______?
   No, I'm not. I'm single.
4. ______?
   I'm a banker.
5. ______?
   Yes. It's very interesting.

C Match each question to an answer. Write the letter.

1. How old are your grandparents? ______
2. How old is your mother? ______
3. What is her job? ______
4. Is it interesting? ______

a. She's an engineer.
b. They're both 61.
c. Yes, it is.
d. She's 33.

Lesson C GRAMMAR AND VOCABULARY

A Unscramble the sentences and questions.

1. is hot a country Mexico Mexico is a hot country.
2. UK a country is the wet ______________________.
3. continent big Asia a is ______________________?
4. a Saudi Arabia country is dry ______________________?
5. Mexico South America in isn't ______________________.

B Read the answers. Write the questions.

1. Is Belize a big country? No, it isn't. It's a small country.
2. ______________________? Yes, it is. It is a very wet country.
3. ______________________? No, it isn't. It's in South America.
4. ______________________? Yes, it is. It's a very cold country.
5. ______________________? Yes, it is. It's a very dry country.

C Complete the conversation.

Fernando: Where do (1) ______________________ come from, Galina?
Galina: I'm (2) ______________________ Moscow.
Fernando: Moscow is in (3) ______________________, right?
Galina: Yes, it is.
Fernando: So, tell me about Russia, Galina.
Galina: Well, it's in (4) ______________________.
Fernando: (5) ______________________ Russia a cold country?
Galina: Yes, it's (6) ______________________ cold.

D Make a new conversation about your city and your country.

Brandon: Where do you come from?
You: ______________________.
Brandon: ______________________ is in ______________________, right?
You: Yes, it is.
Brandon: So tell me about ______________________.
You: It's in ______________________.

Farmers of the World

Adriano is from Brazil. He is thirty-four years old. He's married with two children, a son and a daughter. Adriano and his wife grow coffee. Their coffee is very, very good. It goes to countries in Europe and North America. The weather in Brazil is great for growing coffee. It is always hot and wet.

Yong-Jun is from Korea. He is twenty-three years old. He is married with one young daughter. Yong-Jun is a farmer, too. He is not a coffee farmer. He is a rice farmer. The rice is for his family and for people in Seoul. The weather in Korea is good for rice. In summer, it is hot and wet. In winter, it is cold and dry.

A Circle **T** for *true* or **F** for *false.*

1. Adriano is from Brazil.	T	F
2. Adriano is married.	T	F
3. Adriano grows rice.	T	F
4. His coffee goes to Europe.	T	F
5. Hot, wet weather is great for growing coffee.	T	F
6. Yong-Jun is from Seoul.	T	F
7. Yong-Jun is single.	T	F
8. Yong-Jun grows rice.	T	F
9. His rice goes to North America.	T	F
10. Summer is hot and dry in Korea.	T	F

B This in Antonio. Write about Antonio. Use the words in the box.

hot Honduras thirty-four married wet
bananas North America Antonio children

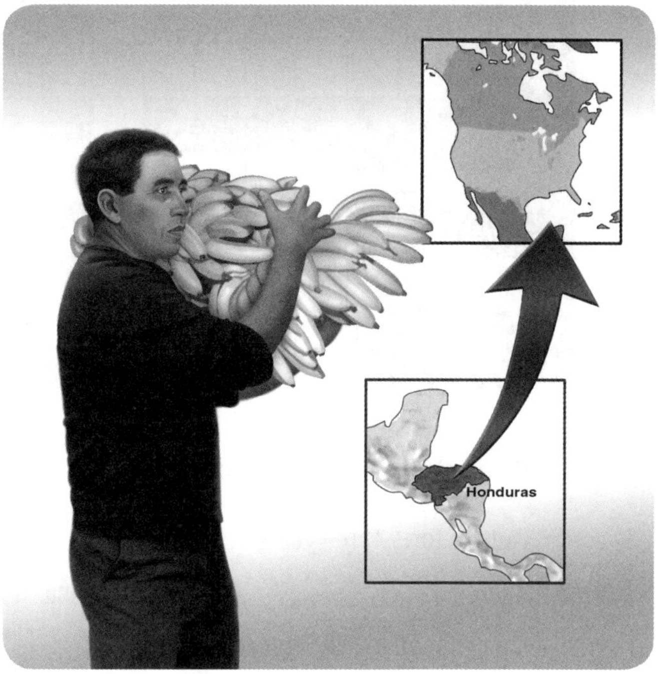

Review

A Solve the crossword puzzle using vocabulary and grammar from this unit.

Across

2. It isn't interesting. It's _______.
3. Egypt is a _______.
4. Seoul is in _______.
6. The United Kingdom is in _______.
8. Africa is a _______.
9. Buenos Aires is in _______.
11. Beijing is in _______.
12. It isn't big. It's _______.
13. He's a taxi _______.

Down

1. Brazil is in _______. (2 words)
5. It isn't dry. It's _______.
7. I'm 19 years _______.
10. She's _______ engineer.
11. It isn't hot. It's _______.

B Complete the description with words from the box.

job in a ~~is~~ teacher dry

Ruth is forty-three years old. She (1) ____is____ from Zambia. Zambia is (2) ____________ Africa. It's (3) ____________ small country. The weather is hot and (4) ____________ in the summer. Ruth is a (5) ____________. Her (6) ____________ is interesting. Ruth is married with two young children.

C Write a description of a friend. Use words from the unit.

____

____

____

____

____

HOUSES AND APARTMENTS

Lesson A GRAMMAR AND VOCABULARY

A Label the pictures.

kitchen dining room living room garage stairs bathroom bedroom closet

1. ______________

2. ______________

3. ______________

4. ______________

5. ______________

6. ______________

7. ______________

8. ______________

B Complete the conversation. Circle the correct option.

Realtor: This house isn't big, but it's very nice. (1) (There is | There are) two bedrooms, and (2) (there is | is there) a nice living room.

Mr. Chang: (3) (There are | Are there) closets in the bedrooms?

Realtor: Yes, (4) (there is | there are). And (5) (there are | there is) a big kitchen.

Mr. Chang: That's good. (6) (Is there | there is) a garage?

Realtor: No, (7) (there is | there isn't). But (8) (there is | there isn't) a beautiful garden.

C Write questions using the words given. Then write answers about where you live.

1. (two bathrooms) *Are there two bathrooms in your house?*
   Yes, there are. OR No, there aren't.
2. (a garden) ______________________________
   ____
3. (a living room) ______________________________
   ____
4. (closets) ______________________________
   ____

Lesson B GRAMMAR AND VOCABULARY

A Change the sentences. Make them plural.

1. There is *one* bedroom in his apartment. (two)
   There are two bedrooms in his apartment.
2. There is *one* closet in my house. (three)
   ______________________________.
3. There is *one* bathroom in her house. (two)
   ______________________________.
4. There is *one* garage in their house. (two)
   ______________________________.

B Say the plural words from exercise **A.** Write them in the correct column.

Ends in /s/ sound	Ends in /z/ sound	Ends in /iz/ sound

C Describe these homes. Use your ideas.

1. a. bedrooms There are ten bedrooms in this house.
   b. bathrooms ______________________________
   c. closets ______________________________
   d. garage ______________________________
   e. swimming pool ______________________________
   f. (your own idea) ______________________________

2. a. bedrooms ______________________________
   b. bathrooms ______________________________
   c. garden ______________________________
   d. living room ______________________________
   e. swimming pool ______________________________
   f. (your own idea) ______________________________

Lesson C GRAMMAR AND VOCABULARY

A Label the things in the apartment.

microwave ~~sofa~~ bed table stove
armchair coffee table lamp refrigerator
chair TV bookcase

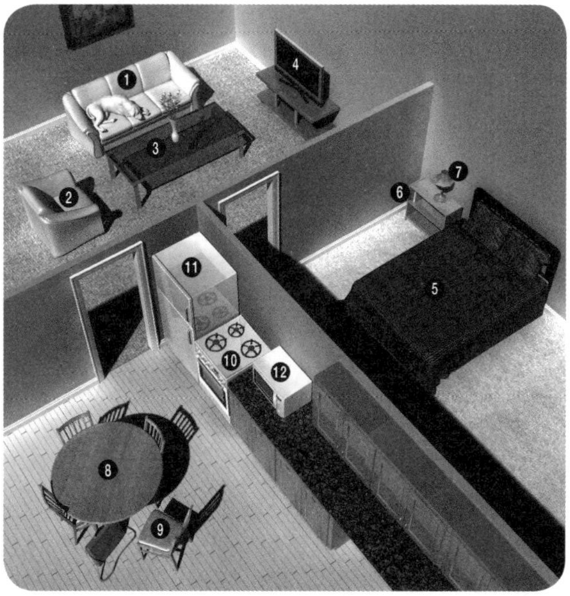

1. sofa
2. ____
3. ____
4. ____
5. ____
6. ____
7. ____
8. ____
9. ____
10. ____
11. ____
12. ____

B Look at the picture in exercise **A.** Complete the sentences with *in, on, under,* or *next to.*

1. The dog is on the sofa.
2. The bookcase is ____ the bed.
3. The picture is ____ the living room wall.
4. The TV is ____ the living room.
5. The coffee table is ____ the flowers.
6. The refrigerator is ____ the stove.

C Complete the conversation with *in, on, under,* or *next to.* Use each preposition once.

A: Where is my cell phone?

B: Is it ____ the kitchen?

A: No, it isn't.

B: Is it ____ my phone ____ the table?

A: No, it isn't!

B: Here it is! It's ____ the sofa!

D Complete the sentences about your house or apartment.

1. ____ is next to ____.
2. ____ is in ____.
3. ____ is on ____.
4. The ____ is in ____.

What's in Your Bedroom?

My name is Yoshi. I'm from Nagoya, in Japan. This is my bedroom. It's small, but there are two closets and a big window. There isn't a bed. There is a *futon*—it's a Japanese bed. The *futon* is in the closet during the day, but it is next to the window during the night. There is a small table for my books, but there isn't a chair. I sit on the floor.

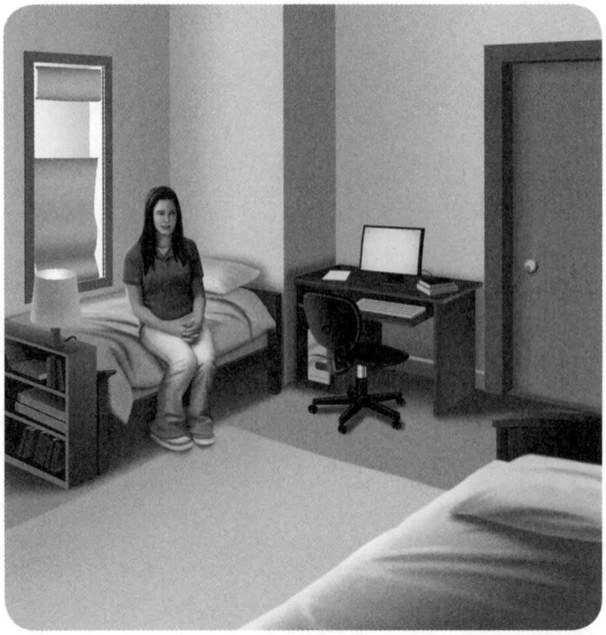

I'm Jessie. I'm from Los Angeles, in the United States. My sister and I have a bedroom together. There are two beds. Her bed is next to the door, and my bed is under the window. There's a bookcase with many books and a lamp. The computer table and chair are next to my bed. Our bedroom isn't big, but it's very nice.

A Check (✓) all the correct answers.

	Yoshi's bedroom	Jessie's bedroom
1. There is a table.	✓	✓
2. There are two beds.		
3. There are books.		
4. It's small.		
5. There is a chair.		
6. There is a window.		

B Draw a picture of your bedroom.

C Write about the things in your bedroom.

Review

A Solve the crossword puzzle using vocabulary and grammar from this unit.

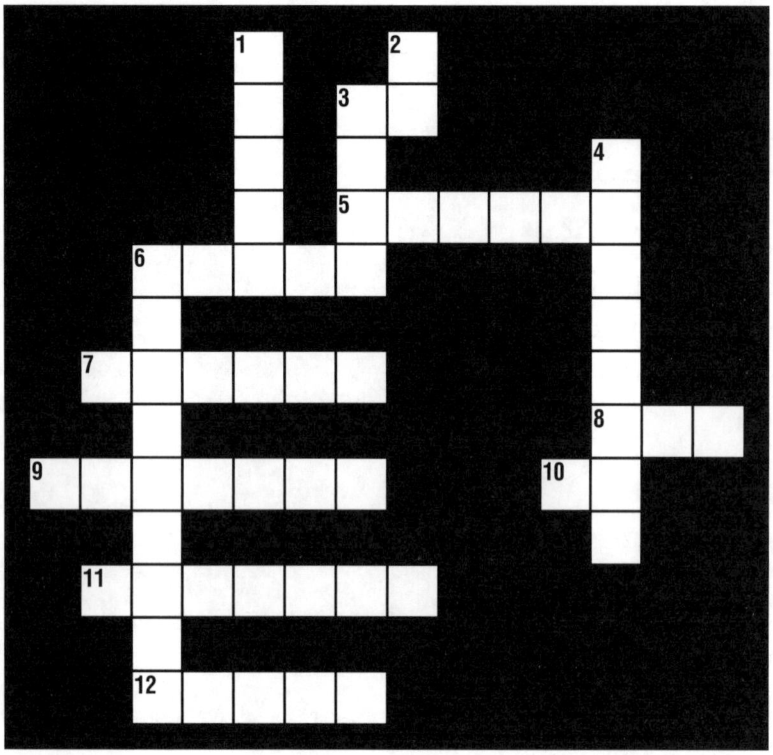

Across

3. The table is ______ the dining room.
5. The bookcase is ______ the door. (2 words)
6. "Are there windows in your kitchen?" "No, there ______."
7. The car is in the ______.
8. There ______ two armchairs in the living room.
9. The stove is in the ______.
10. There ______ a sofa in the living room.
11. The bed is in the ______.
12. Is ______ a coffee table in your living room?

Down

1. There are three bedrooms in my ______.
2. The flowers are ______ the table.
3. "Is there a TV in your bedroom?" "No, there ______."
4. The books are in the ______.
6. I don't have a house. I have an ______.

B Complete the paragraph with words from the box.

there is	in	under
dining room	big	
there are	~~living room~~	
there isn't		

This is my (1) ___living room___. It's a (2) ______________ room and (3) ______________ a big window. (4) ______________ two sofas and an armchair. The sofa is (5) ______________ the window. (6) ______________ a table. The table is (7) ______________ the (8) ______________.

POSSESSIONS

UNIT 4

Lesson A GRAMMAR AND VOCABULARY

A Unscramble the possessions.

1. okbo b________
2. koontobe n________
3. yardinocti d________
4. ginr r________
5. lacknece n________
6. tallwe w________
7. gba b________
8. syek k________
9. chatw w________
10. sssalge g________
11. kkaaccbp b________
12. pne p________

B Complete the sentences with *this, that, these,* or *those.* Use the hints in parentheses.

1. (far) That is my bag.
2. (near) ________ are my glasses.
3. (near) ________ is my dictionary.
4. (far) ________ are my notebooks.
5. (near) ________ are my keys.
6. (far) ________ is my ring.

C Read the questions and complete the answers.

1. Is that your backpack? No, it isn't.
2. Are these your glasses? Yes, ________.
3. Is this your pen? Yes, ________.
4. Are those your keys? No, ________.
5. Is that your dictionary? Yes, ________.

D Look at the picture. Write questions with *this, that, these,* and *those.*

1. keys ________
2. dictionary ________
3. books ________
4. glasses ________
5. bag ________
6. wallet ________
7. notebook ________
8. watch ________

Lesson B GRAMMAR AND VOCABULARY

A Read the chart. Complete the sentences with possessive nouns.

	Paul	Francisco	Jennie
car	Toyota	Ford	Kia
house	1 bedroom, 1 bathroom	6 bedrooms, 4 bathrooms	3 bedrooms, 1 bathroom
dog	name: Blackie	name: Missie	name: Max

1. Jennie's dog is Max.
2. ______________ house is very big.
3. ______________ car is Japanese.
4. ______________ house is small.
5. ______________ dog is Missie.
6. ______________ car is Korean.

B Look at the picture of Anita and her brother Martin. Write sentences with *this, that, these,* and *those.*

1. keys/Anita These are Anita's keys.
2. car/Anita ______________
3. glasses/Martin ______________
4. handbag/Anita ______________
5. book/Martin ______________
6. wallet/Anita ______________
7. house/Martin ______________

C Write lists.

1. What's in your bag?

______________ ______________ ______________

______________ ______________ ______________

______________ ______________ ______________

2. What's on your desk?

______________ ______________ ______________

______________ ______________ ______________

______________ ______________ ______________

Lesson C GRAMMAR AND VOCABULARY

A Label the pictures.

camcorder smartphone MP3 player speakers tablet DVD player cell phone laptop

1. ____________

2. ____________

3. ____________

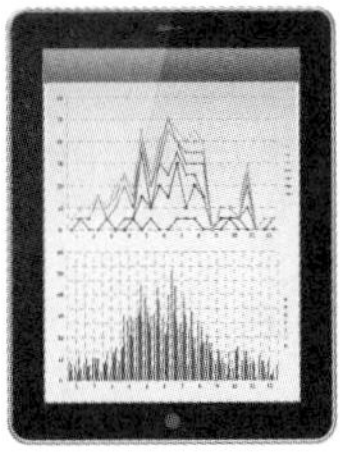

4. ____________

5. ____________

6. ____________

7. ____________

8. ____________

B Write short answers that are true for you.

1. Do you have a tablet? Yes, I do. OR No, I don't.
2. Does your teacher have glasses? ____________
3. Do your friends have tablets? ____________
4. Do you have a DVD player? ____________
5. Do your father and mother have a camcorder? ____________
6. Do you have a smartphone? ____________

C Complete the conversation.

Cherie: (1) ________ you have a laptop?

Mia: Yes, (2) ________ ________. It's great. It's in my bag.

Cherie: And do (3) ________ ________ a tablet?

Mia: Yes. This tablet (4) ________ music, games, and videos. It's really cool.

Cherie: Wow! What about a camera? (5) ________ ________ ________ a camera?

Mia: No, (6) ________ ________. But I (7) ________ a cell phone. And my tablet (8) ________ a camera, too.

Special Possessions

A Read about these special possessions.

Maite:

I have a very pretty necklace. It's my mother's necklace from Mexico. It's made of silver. My family is from Mexico, and the necklace is very old—about 100 years old! This necklace is my special possession.

Andy:

My special possession is a picture. All the members of my family are in the picture: my grandfather, my grandmother, my father, my mother, and all my brothers and sisters and their families. The picture is two years old. I have the picture in my living room now.

Bella:

I have one very special possession. It's my camera. It's new, and it's very small. It's a very good camera, and it isn't cheap! I take pictures of my friends and family. I always have my camera in my bag!

B Circle **T** for *true* or **F** for *false.*

1. Maite's family is from Mexico.	T	F
2. Bella's camera is small.	T	F
3. Maite's necklace is made of gold.	T	F
4. Andy's family is big.	T	F
5. Andy's picture is old.	T	F
6. Bella's special possession is a picture.	T	F

C Write these sentences again. Use capital letters and punctuation.

my special possession is a watch it's very big and old it's gold it's special because it's my grandfather's watch and it's 100 years old

D Write about a special possession that you have. What is it? Is it old or new? Is it big or small? Why is it special?

Review

A Solve the crossword puzzle with grammar and vocabulary from this unit.

Down

1. My ______ is English and Spanish.
2. a DVD ______
3. a small computer
4. We ______ a tablet.
5. ______ she have a car?
8. "Is that your bag?" "No, it ______."
12. David ______ a smartphone.

Across

1. ______ you have a cell phone?
6. "Are these your glasses?" "No, they ______."
7. My money is in my ______.
9. things you have
10. "Do you have a camera?" "______, I don't."
11. That camera is $20. It's ______.
13. "Do you have a car?" "______, I do."

B Complete the paragraph with words from the box.

but	have	or	~~has~~	and

My sister (1) __has__ a smartphone and an MP3 player (2) ______________ I don't. My brother is a banker. He has a smartphone, a laptop, (3) ______________ a tablet. I don't have a smartphone, an MP3 player, a laptop, (4) ______________ a tablet! I only (5) ______________ an old cell phone.

C Write about what possessions you and your family have. Use words from the unit.

____

____

____

____

____

DAILY ACTIVITIES

Lesson A GRAMMAR AND VOCABULARY

A What time is it? Write the time.

1. 4:45 It's a quarter to five.
2. 11:00 ______________________
3. 7:30 ______________________
4. 9:15 ______________________
5. 2:30 ______________________
6. Now ______________________

B What time do you do these things? Write sentences.

1. I start work at eight o'clock.

2. ______________________

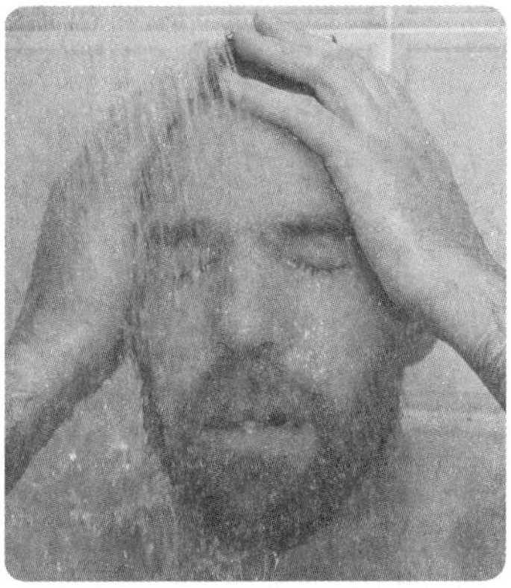

3. ______________________

4. ______________________

5. ______________________

6. ______________________

C Complete the time expression by writing the correct word: *in, on, at, every.*

1. I take a nap ______________________ afternoon.
2. Sara has English class ______________________ nine thirty.
3. I do my homework ______________________ the evening.
4. We don't work ______________________ Sundays.
5. I get up ______________________ a quarter to eight.

D Write the verb. Remember *-s* for *he* and *she.*

1. I ______ get ______ up every day at six o'clock.
2. He ______________________ a shower every morning.
3. They ______________________ work at eight thirty in the morning.
4. She ______________________ lunch at one o'clock at school.
5. My father ______________________ work at seven o'clock in the evening.
6. I ______________________ to bed at eleven o'clock.
7. My baby ______________________ a nap in the afternoon.

Lesson B GRAMMAR AND VOCABULARY

A Write the days on the calendar.

Tuesday Friday Saturday Monday Wednesday Thursday

May 1	May 2	May 3	May 4	May 5	May 6	May 7
Sunday	______	______	______	______	______	______

B Look at the information. Write questions and answers.

	Michael
job	chef
get up	10:00
start work	11:00
eat lunch	4:00
finish work	9:00
go to bed	1:30

Michael

1. (job) What's his job?
He's a chef.

2. (get up) What time does he get up?
He gets up at ten o'clock.

3. (start work) ______________________________?
______________________________.

4. (eat lunch) ______________________________?
______________________________.

5. (eat dinner) ______________________________?
______________________________.

6. (finish work) ______________________________?
______________________________.

7. (go to bed) ______________________________?
______________________________.

Lesson C GRAMMAR AND VOCABULARY

A Match the columns.

1. meet ____	**4.** make ____	**a.** the bank	**d.** clients
2. go ____	**5.** go to ____	**b.** to meetings	**e.** reports
3. talk ____	**6.** write ____	**c.** photocopies	**f.** to people on the phone

B Write questions and answers about these people's jobs.

	Dennis and Susan flight attendants	**Melissa** doctor
1. travel	yes	no
2. talk to people	yes	yes
3. go to meetings	no	yes

Dennis and Susan

1. Do Dennis and Susan travel?____?
   Yes, they ____________
2. ______________________?
   ____
3. ______________________?
   ____

Melissa

1. ______________________?
   ____
2. ______________________?
   ____
3. ______________________?
   ____

C Write sentences about what you do. Use *sometimes*, *always*, or *never*.

1. (check my e-mail in the morning)
   ____
2. (go to meetings)
   ____
3. (travel)
   ____
4. (make photocopies)
   ____
5. (write reports)
   ____

A Dog's Work

A Read the article. Write the number of the picture.

1\.

2\.

3\.

Dogs look for bombs. They also look for dangerous things in people's bags. It's a hard, dangerous job for people, but it's easy for dogs. *Picture* ______

Dogs work on farms. They help the farmers with the animals. Their working hours are very long, and their salary is $0. *Picture* ______

Dogs help blind people. They go to meetings with people. They go to the bank with people—they help with many things every day. *Picture* ______

Dogs like work. For a dog, a job is interesting and important.

B Circle **T** for *true* or **F** for *false.*

1. Dogs help people at meetings. T F
2. Dogs sometimes work with animals on farms. T F
3. Dogs sometimes do dangerous work. T F
4. Dogs have a salary. T F
5. Dogs like their jobs. T F
6. Farm dogs don't work long hours. T F
7. Dogs look for dangerous things. T F
8. Dogs' jobs aren't important. T F

C Complete the sentences.

~~easy~~ sometimes early to and every

A teacher's work isn't ___easy___. Teachers start work __________ in the morning. They teach classes __________ day. They help their students, and they go __________ meetings. They always read a lot of books __________ papers. They __________ work in the evening, too. But it's a good and important job.

D Write about a job you know.

____

____

____

____

____

____

____

____

UNIT 5

Review

A Solve the crossword puzzle with grammar and vocabulary from this unit.

Across

2. I get up _______ seven o'clock.
3. I _______ people on the phone every day. (2 words)
5. I _______ a nap in the afternoon.
6. _______ time do you start work?
9. I _______ travel for my job.
12. I _______ to bed at eleven o'clock.

Down

1. At work, I _______ clients.
2. things that you do
4. I see my friends _______ Saturdays.
7. I _______ dinner with my family.
8. At work, I _______ reports.
10. I finish work at five _______.
11. I take a shower _______ day.

B Complete the paragraph with words from the box.

talks	always	starts
in	writes	~~every day~~
at	bed	

My mother gets up early (1) ___every day___. She's a nurse and she (2) _______________ work at 7:30 a.m. She (3) _______________ takes a shower (4) _______________ night, and she goes to (5) _______________ at 10 o'clock (6) _______________ the evening. She likes her job. At work, she (7) _______________ to people every day, and she sometimes (8) _______________ reports.

C Write about your, or someone in your family's, daily activities. Use words from the unit.

____

____

____

____

GETTING THERE

UNIT 6

Lesson A GRAMMAR AND VOCABULARY

A Label the pictures.

tourist office	train station	supermarket	post office	library	park
restaurant	hotel	museum	bus station	movie theater	bank

1. ____________

2. ____________

3. ____________

4. ____________

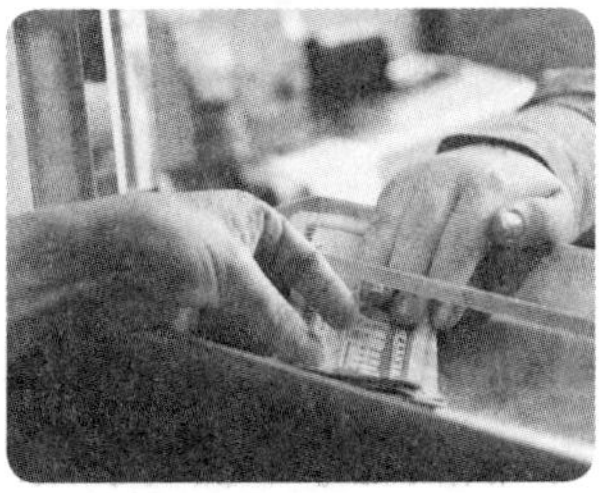

5. ____________

6. ____________

7. ____________

8. ____________

9. ____________

10. ____________

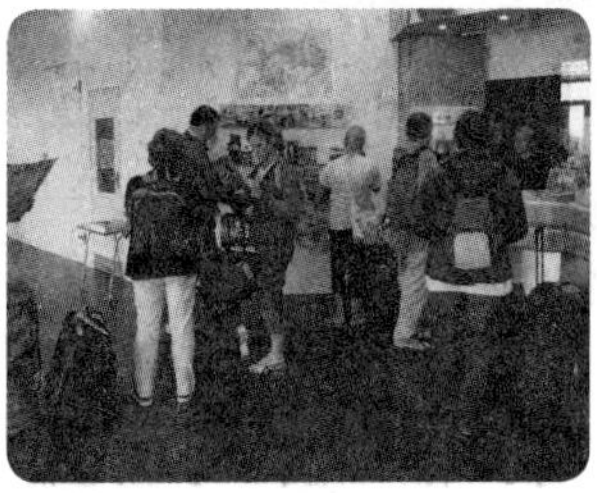

11. ____________

12. ____________

B Read the directions and circle the correct word in parentheses.

There's a good restaurant near my school. It's (in | on) the corner of Center Street and Linden Avenue. Leave the school and (turn | get) left. Then (walk | take) two blocks. Pizza House is across (from | with) the park. It's (between | on) the supermarket and the movie theater.

C Write directions to a place near your school.

There's a/an ______________________ near my school. ______________________

____

____

____

Lesson B GRAMMAR AND VOCABULARY

Look at the map. Complete the conversations.

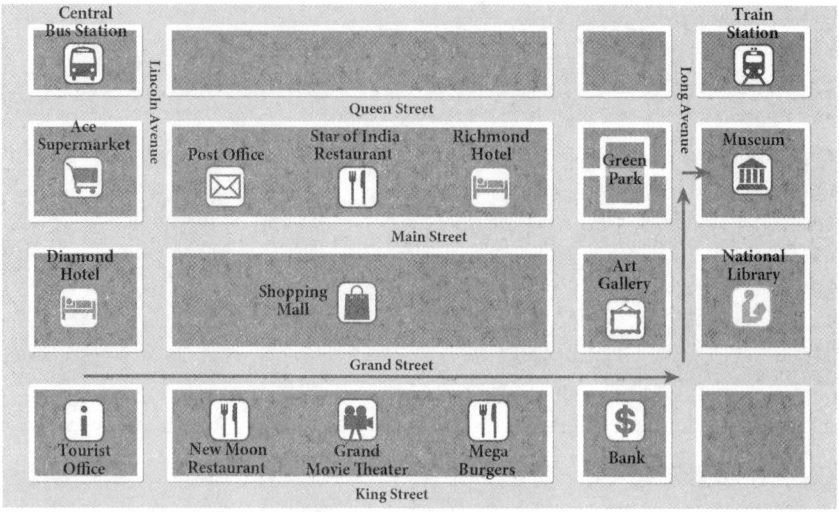

A You are at the Diamond Hotel. You need a post office.

You: Is there a post office near here?

Receptionist: Yes, there is. It's on (1) ____________ next to (2) ____________.

You: How (3) ____________ get there?

Receptionist: Leave the hotel and turn (4) ____________. Walk (5) ____________. It's on the corner of (6) ____________ and (7) ____________.

You: (8) ____________ you for your help.

Receptionist: You're welcome.

B You are at the museum. You need a bank.

You: (1) ____________ near here?

Employee: Yes, there is. It's on the corner of (2) ____________ and (3) ____________.

You: How do I get there?

Employee: Leave the museum and (4) ____________ left then right. Walk (5) ____________. It's across from (6) ____________.

You: Thank you.

Employee: You're welcome.

C You are at the tourist office. Use your own idea.

You: Is there ____________?

Employee: ____________

You: ____________

Employee: ____________

____

____

You: ____________

Lesson C GRAMMAR AND VOCABULARY

A Label the symbols for transportation.

subway bus train taxi rental car

1. ______________

2. ______________

3. ______________

4. ______________

5. ______________

B Read the chart. Complete the sentences with the correct form of *have to.*

To the airport	🕓	$	bags
train	50 minutes	$9	1 bag
subway (change one time)	1 hour 20 minutes	$3	1 bag
taxi	20 minutes	$35	2 bags
airport shuttle bus	1 hour 30 minutes	$12	2 bags
bus (change two times)	3 hours	$8	1 bag
rental car	30 minutes	$79	5 bags

1. Mr. Davis has four bags. He ______________________ rent a car.
2. Teresa needs to be at the airport in one hour. She has two bags. She ______________________ take a taxi.
3. On the subway, you ______________________ change one time. If you take the train, you ______________________ change.
4. Jeff doesn't have much money. He ______________________ take the bus.
5. Lina can take the bus to the airport. She ______________________ get there quickly.
6. Hassan needs to be at the airport in two hours. He has two bags. He ______________________ take the airport shuttle bus.

C Write three places in your city. Then write sentences about transportation to them from your school.

1. Place: Metro Department Store
   Transportation: You have to take the 78 bus.
2. Place: ____
   Transportation: ____
3. Place: ____
   Transportation: ____

My Travel Diary: Japan

A Read the diary of a trip. Write the dates by the pictures.

August 1 I come to Tokyo. I'm in Japan for two weeks. It's beautiful, but it's so expensive! I want to visit many cities. In Tokyo, I take the subway. It's very fast.

August 4 I walk up Mount Fuji with my Japanese friends. It's very cold at the top, but beautiful.

August 6 I take a very fast train to Osaka. In Osaka, I visit the Museum of History and the aquarium. They're very interesting.

August 10 I go to Shikoku Island on a boat. Shikoku is green and beautiful.

August 13 I take the night bus to the city of Fukuoka. The bus is very cheap, so I have money for dinner in a nice restaurant.

August 15 Today is my last day. I take a shuttle bus to the airport. Goodbye to Japan!

1. ______________

2. ______________

3. ______________

4. ______________

5. ______________

6. ______________

B Circle **T** for *true* or **F** for *false*.

1. The man is in Tokyo for two weeks.	T	F
2. The subway in Tokyo is fast.	T	F
3. The man goes to a nice restaurant in Osaka.	T	F
4. He takes a train to Shikoku.	T	F
5. The bus to Fukuoka is cheap.	T	F
6. He takes the bus to the airport.	T	F

C Write your itinerary for a trip you want to take. Use *first, next, then,* and *finally.*

My Destination: ______________________________

August 1 ______________________________

____

August 6 ______________________________

____

August 10 ______________________________

____

August 13 ______________________________

____

UNIT 6

Review

A Solve the crossword puzzle with grammar and vocabulary from this unit.

Down

1. Ask questions at the tourist ______.
2. Shop at a ______.
4. Take the ______ bus to the airport.
7. The hotel is ______ from the bus station.
8. The movie theater is ______ the museum and the post office.
9. The train ______ is on National Avenue.

Across

3. Walk two ______.
5. You ______ to take the subway.
6. It isn't expensive. It's ______.
11. Eat dinner in a ______.
12. ______ the street
13. It's ______ the corner of King Street and Southern Avenue.

B Write an itinerary for a tourist in your country. Use words from the unit.

FREE TIME

Lesson A GRAMMAR AND VOCABULARY

A Label the activities.

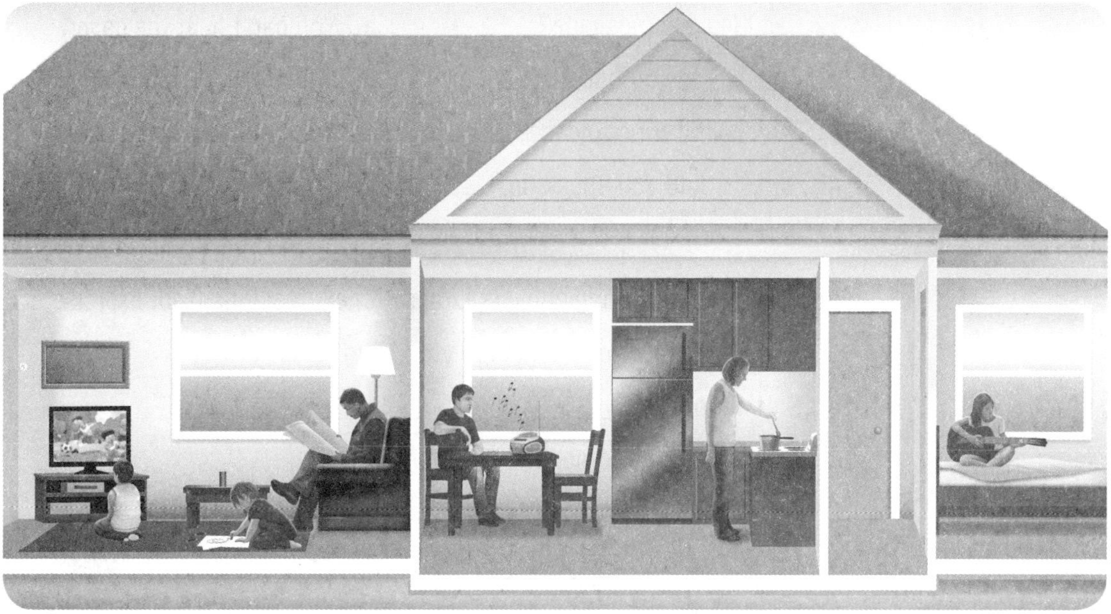

B Write sentences about some of the people in exercise **A**.

1. He's watching TV.
2. ______
3. ______
4. ______
5. ______

C Match the questions and answers.

1. What are you reading? ____
2. Are they going for a walk? ____
3. What is Brandon doing? ____
4. Is Sara cooking lunch? ____
5. Where are you going? ____

a. No, they aren't.
b. Yes, she is.
c. I'm going to my computer class.
d. I'm reading an interesting book.
e. He's watching TV.

Lesson B GRAMMAR AND VOCABULARY

A Match the telephone expressions to the situations.

1. Can I leave a message? ____
2. Could I call you back? ____
3. Who is speaking, please? ____
4. Sorry, could you speak up? ____

a. You can't hear the caller.
b. You are busy and can't talk.
c. You don't know the caller.
d. The person you are calling is not available.

B Complete the telephone conversations with expressions from exercise **A**.

1. **A:** Hi! How are you? What are you doing?
   B: I'm cooking. ________________________________?
   A: Sure, I'm at home. Call me later.
2. **A:** Good afternoon. Can I speak to Mr. Li, please?
   B: ________________________________?
   A: Guey Lan Wu.
   B: I'm sorry, Mr. Li is not here.
   A: ________________________________?
   B: Yes, of course.

C Complete the telephone conversations. Write the verbs in the correct form.

1. **A:** Hi! What _are you doing_ (you/do)?
   B: ______________ (I/go) to the movies with Ana. Come with us!
   A: OK. Thanks!
2. **A:** Hi. How are you?
   B: Oh, hi. Can I call you back? ______________ (I/watch) TV.
   A: Sure, but call me on my cell phone. ______________ (we/go) for a walk.
3. **A:** Hi. I'm at the supermarket. ______________ (you/cooking) dinner today?
   B: Yes, ______________. Buy rice, please.
   A: OK. Bye!

Lesson C GRAMMAR AND VOCABULARY

A Label the sports.

soccer golf swimming volleyball
biking ice skating skiing tennis

1. ______________

2. ______________

3. ______________

4. ______________

5. ______________

6. ______________

7. ______________

8. ______________

B Write sentences about these things in your notebook. Use *can* or *can't.*

cook swim speak Spanish play the guitar ice skate

C Complete the e-mail with *can, can't,* or *can you.*

Dear e-pal,

Hi! It's nice to meet you. My name is Laura Rios. I'm from Miami, Florida, in the United States.

I ______________ speak English and Spanish. We ______________ write e-mails in Spanish if you like.

I love sports. I ______________ play tennis, golf, and soccer. ______________ play any sports? I also like music. I ______________ play the guitar, but I ______________ sing because it's too difficult. I like food, but I ______________ cook very well. I can only make sandwiches. ______________ cook?

Please write me an e-mail!

Your friend,

Laura

Lesson D READING AND WRITING

A Special Race

This man works in a café. He is a waiter. Now he is in a special race. He is walking and carrying a tray of water!

Every year, in Paris, France, there is a race for café waiters. They walk 8 kilometers (5 miles) in the streets of Paris. They carry a tray of drinks. The rules are simple: The waiters can't run—they can only walk. They can't drink the drinks. And they can't drop their tray.

More than 500 people are in the race, and many other people watch the race.

Sometimes, waiters come from other countries to be in the Paris race. There are also waiters' races in different cities around the world, like Washington D.C., Sydney, and London.

A Read the article. Circle **T** for *true* and **F** for *false*. Correct the false sentences.

1. The race is in ~~England~~.	T	(F)	France
2. The race is for café waiters.	T	F	________
3. The waiters run in the race.	T	F	________
4. The race is in the street.	T	F	________
5. The race is 5 kilometers.	T	F	________
6. There are more than 500 people in the race.	T	F	________
7. Waiters come from other countries for the race.	T	F	________
8. There are now races in other countries.	T	F	________

B Read the questionnaire. Write sentences about you and someone in your family, or a friend.

	Jason	You	______
languages 	I can speak Japanese and English. I can speak a little Spanish.		
sports 	I can swim, and I can play tennis. But I can't play soccer.		
cooking 	I can make sandwiches. But I can't cook.		
art 	I can draw a little, and I can take photos. I can't paint.		

Review

A Solve the crossword puzzle with vocabulary and grammar from this unit.

Across

3. No, I ______ play football.
5. She's ______ to music.
9. Can you ______ golf?
10. Can you ______ skate?
11. We're ______ TV.
12. "Can they ski?" "Yes, ______." (2 words)

Down

1. "Is he reading?" "Yes, ______." (2 words)
2. "Are they cooking?" " No, ______." (2 words)
3. ______ you play soccer?
4. I'm ______ the guitar.
6. "Can you swim?" "No, ______." (2 words)
7. They're ______ for a walk.
8. ______ is he going?
11. ______ are you doing now?

B Complete the e-mail with words from the box.

studying	listening		
can	~~are~~	can't	can

Hey, Kris! How are you? What (1) ___*are*___ you doing? I'm (2) ______________ and (3) ______________ to some really cool music. (4) ______________ you play the guitar? I (5) ______________. :(. But I (6) ______________ sing :) .

Call me later!

Nuri

C Write an e-mail to a friend about what you are doing now and what you can or can't do. Use words from the unit.

____

____

____

____

CLOTHES

UNIT 8

Lesson A GRAMMAR AND VOCABULARY

A Label the clothes in the picture.

pants	dress	shirt	jacket
shoes	hat	sweater	coat

B Unscramble the colors.

1. dre ____________________
2. tehiw ____________________
3. calkb ____________________
4. norbw ____________________
5. lowley ____________________
6. naogre ____________________
7. nerge ____________________
8. uble ____________________

C Complete the conversation with the words in the box.

try could of course small sweaters

Customer: Do you have any blue ____________________?

Sales Assistant: Yes, we do.

Customer: ____________________ I see them, please?

Sales Assistant: Sure.

Customer: These look nice. Could I ____________ them on?

Sales Assistant: Yes, ____________________. What size?

Customer: ____________________, please.

D Write a new conversation. Use your own ideas.

Customer: Do you have any ____________________?

Sales Assistant: ____________________

Customer: ____________________

Sales Assistant: ____________________

Customer: ____________________

Sales Assistant: ____________________

Customer: ____________________

Lesson B GRAMMAR AND VOCABULARY

A Unscramble the questions and statements.

1. size you are what What size are you ________________?
2. price $29.99 sale is the ________________.
3. it is much how ________________?
4. have in you this do red ________________?
5. $29.99 that's total ________________.

B Match the questions to the answers. Write the letter.

1. Do you have this in blue? ______
2. How much is it? ______
3. Can I help you?______
4. What size are you? ______
5. Do you want to pay by cash or credit card? ______

a. Yes, I'm looking for a hat.
b. I'm a 10.
c. I'll pay by credit card.
d. Yes, we do.
e. The sale price is $19.99.

C Complete the conversation with expressions from the box.

What size are you
How much is it
I'm looking for
~~Can I help you~~
that's $49 total
The sale price is
Do you want to pay by cash or credit card

Sales assistant: (1) Can I help you ________________?
Customer: Yes, (2) ________________ a black jacket.
Sales assistant: OK. (3) ________________?
Customer: I'm an 8.
Sales Assistant: OK, here you are.
Customer: (4) ________________?
Sales Assistant: (5) ________________ $49.
Customer: Can I try it on, please?
Sales Assistant: Of course.
Customer: It fits great. I'll take it!
Sales Assistant: OK. (6) ________________?
Customer: Cash.
Sales Assistant: OK, (7)________________. Thank you very much.
Customer: Thank you.

Lesson C GRAMMAR AND VOCABULARY

A What color do you think these things are? Write the color.

red purple beige orange ~~light green~~ dark green light blue dark blue

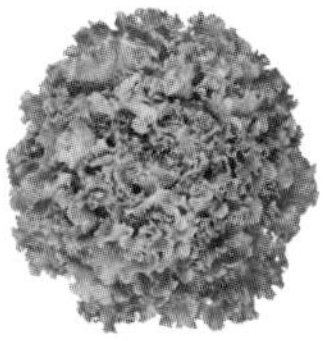

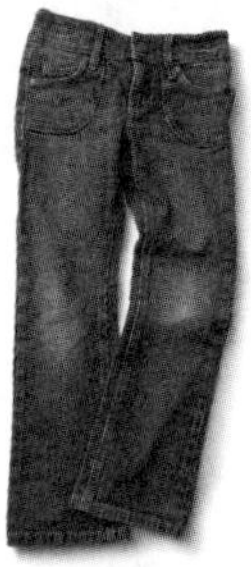

1. It's light green.
2. They're __________.
3. It's __________.
4. They're __________.

5. They're __________.
6. It's __________.
7. They're __________.
8. It's __________.

B Write the correct word from the box.

jeans socks blouse scarf T-shirt

1. It's a kind of shirt with a picture or words on it. __________
2. You wear these with shoes. __________
3. They're a kind of pants. They're usually blue or black. __________
4. You wear it in cold weather. __________
5. It's a kind of shirt for women. __________

C What do you think about these things? Write sentences with *like, love, don't like,* or *hate.*

1. black jeans I don't like black jeans.
2. casual clothes __________
3. T-shirts with words __________
4. sneakers __________

D Write sentences with the verbs. Use your own ideas.

1. (love) I love __________
2. (like) __________
3. (don't like) __________
4. (hate) __________

Your Fashion Store

A Read the information from the Web site. Write the number of the picture that matches each description.

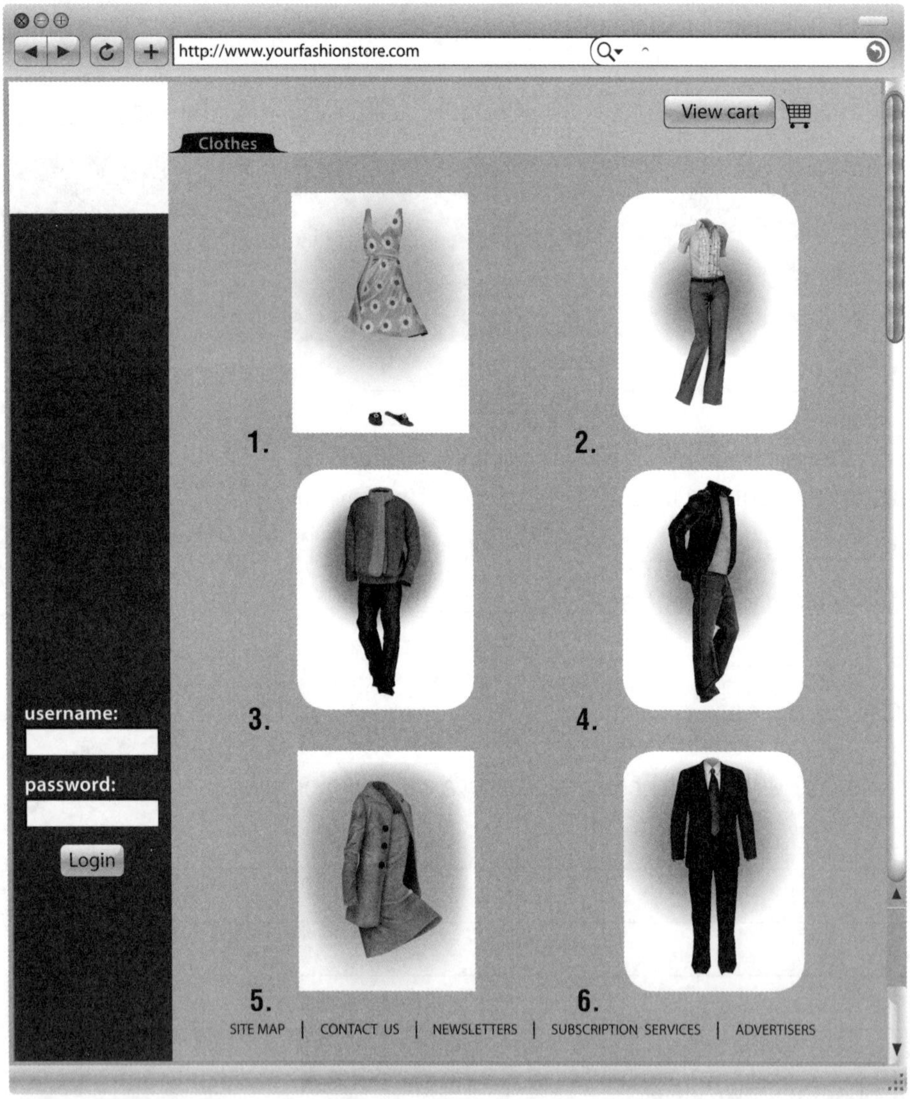

a. You look casual in a T-shirt, jeans, and black jacket. All for just $175. *Picture* ____

b. On cold winter days, you need these pants with a sweater and a scarf. Only $85. *Picture* ____

c. We have this coat and dress in five great colors. Just $125. *Picture* ____

d. The pants, shirt, jacket, and tie look great at your office. On sale for $250. *Picture* ____

e. Wear this blouse and pants to your next party. Only $99. *Picture* ____

f. This dress and shoes are perfect for a hot summer day. Just $79. *Picture* ____

B Look at the pictures and complete the descriptions with words from the box.

looks is wearing ~~casual~~ good shopping beige light informal T-shirt

Picture 1. Toni is wearing (1) casual clothes. She (2) ______________ dark blue jeans and a gray (3) ______________. I think she's going (4) ______________. She (5) ______________ very comfortable.

Picture 2. Max is wearing (6) ______________ clothes. He's wearing (7) ______________ pants and a (8) ______________ blue sweater. I think he's going to a restaurant with his family. He looks (9) ______________.

Toni

Max

C Write a description of a friend or family member. Use the questions to help you:

What is he/she wearing? What color is it? How does he/she look? Do you like it? Where is he/she going?

____

____

____

____

____

____

____

UNIT 8

Review

A Solve the crossword puzzle with vocabulary and grammar from this unit.

Across

5. ______ open the window, please? (2 words)
9. Yes, of ______.
10. Can I ______ on these shoes?
11. A sales ______ works in a store.
12. Yellow and white are ______ colors.

Down

1. He is paying for his clothes by credit ______.
2. a shirt for women
3. You wear a ______ in cold weather.
4. It isn't light blue. It's ______ blue.
5. make something different
6. I like T-shirts a lot. I ______ T-shirts.
7. She's ______ a dress.
8. Jeans and T-shirts are ______ clothes.
13. I don't like ties. I ______ ties.

B Write a description of what you are wearing now and say what clothes you love, like, dislike, and hate. Use words from the unit.

____

____

____

____

____

EAT WELL

UNIT 9

Lesson A GRAMMAR AND VOCABULARY

A Label the food in the pictures.

milk and cereal	coffee	eggs	fish
chocolate cake	salad	pasta	chicken
ice cream	steak	tea	fruit juice

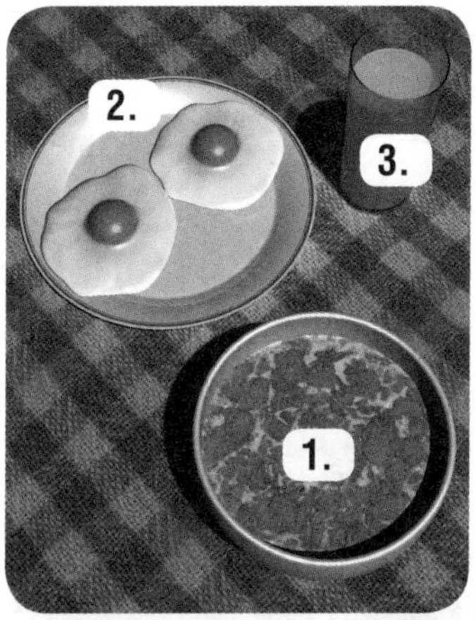

1. ________
2. ________
3. ________

4. ________
5. ________
6. ________
7. ________
8. ________

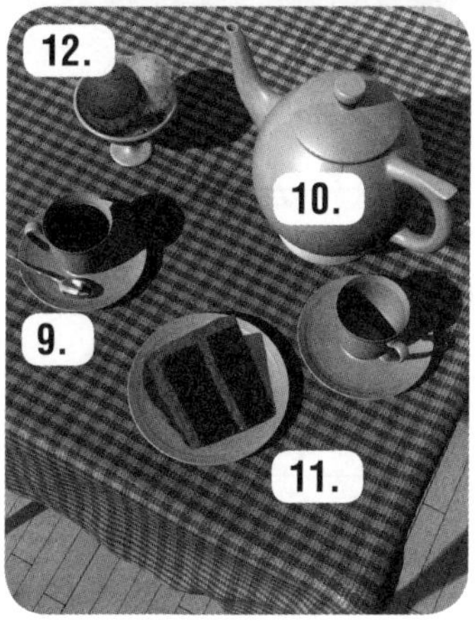

9. ________
10. ________
11. ________
12. ________

B Complete the sentences with *some* or *any*.

1. Please buy ________ ice cream at the supermarket.
2. Do you have ________ fruit juice?
3. There isn't ________ pasta.
4. Do you want ________ coffee?
5. There is ________ chocolate cake in the refrigerator.
6. Is there ________ salad.
7. Can I have ________ tea, please?
8. I can't make a cake. We don't have ________ eggs.

C Complete the conversation with *some* or *any.*

Waiter: Good morning.

Customer: Could I have ________ tea, please?

Waiter: Sure.

Customer: Do you have ________ chocolate cake?

Waiter: No, I'm sorry. We don't have ________ chocolate cake. We only have strawberry cake.

Customer: OK, I'll have ________ strawberry cake.

D Write a new conversation. Use foods you like.

Waiter: ______________________________.

You: ______________________________.

Waiter: ______________________________.

You: ______________________________.

Waiter: ______________________________.

You: ______________________________.

Lesson B GRAMMAR AND VOCABULARY

A Plan a dinner party! Decide who to invite. You can invite three classmates and three famous people.

Classmates

1. ____________________
2. ____________________
3. ____________________

Famous People

1. ____________________
2. ____________________
3. ____________________

B What food will you serve? Use foods from Lesson **A.**

Menu

Food:

1. ____________________
2. ____________________
3. ____________________
4. ____________________

Drinks:

1. ____________________
2. ____________________
3. ____________________

C Write a shopping list for the dinner party. Use some of the words in the box.

some	loaf of	bottle of
bag of	carton of	box of

1. ____________________
2. ____________________
3. ____________________
4. ____________________
5. ____________________

D Complete the invitation.

You're invited!
Please come to a dinner party at my house! The party is on ____________________ (date), at ____________________ (time). My address is ____________________, and my phone number is ____________________.
See you then!
____________________ (your name)

Lesson C GRAMMAR AND VOCABULARY

A What's on the table? Write the item in the correct column.

Count nouns	Non-count nouns
	some milk

B What's in your refrigerator now? Write eight things. Label them **C** (count noun) or **NC** (non-count).

________ ________ ________ ________

________ ________ ________ ________

C Write questions. Use *how much* or *how many.*

1. She needs some oranges.
   How many oranges does she need?
2. I eat a lot of meat.
   ____
3. He drinks a lot of coffee.
   ____
4. She eats fruit.
   ____
5. We need some eggs.
   ____
6. I drink a lot of tea.
   ____

Lesson D READING AND WRITING

Happy Birthday!

A Read the article.

pie

soup

noodles

Birthday food is different in different countries.

In the United States, people eat cake at birthday parties. They sing and make a wish. They sometimes eat ice cream with the cake.

In Russia, people also have birthday parties, but they don't eat cake. They eat a special pie for their birthday. The pie says "Happy Birthday" on it.

In the Philippines, people eat birthday cake. They also eat pasta on their birthday—special long noodles so they will have a long life.

In Korea, all people have their birthday on New Year's Day. They eat special rice-cake soup on January 1, and they are one year older!

B Check ✓ the correct column for birthday foods in each country.

	United States	Russia	Philippines	Korea
cake				
soup				
pie				
ice cream				
pasta				

C Circle **T** for *true* or **F** for *false.*

1. In the United States, people eat pie and cake on their birthday. T F
2. It says "Happy Birthday" on the rice cakes in Korea. T F
3. In the Philippines, they eat long noodles on their birthday to live a long life. T F
4. In Korea, some people have their birthday on New Year's Day. T F

D Write the paragraph again. Add capital letters and punctuation.

i like my birthday my mother makes a great dinner with my favorite food we eat steak and rice she makes a chocolate cake we sing happy birthday we eat a lot of cake and ice cream

____

____

____

____

____

E Write about your birthday.

____

____

____

____

____

____

____

UNIT 9

Review

A Solve the crossword puzzle with vocabulary and grammar from this unit.

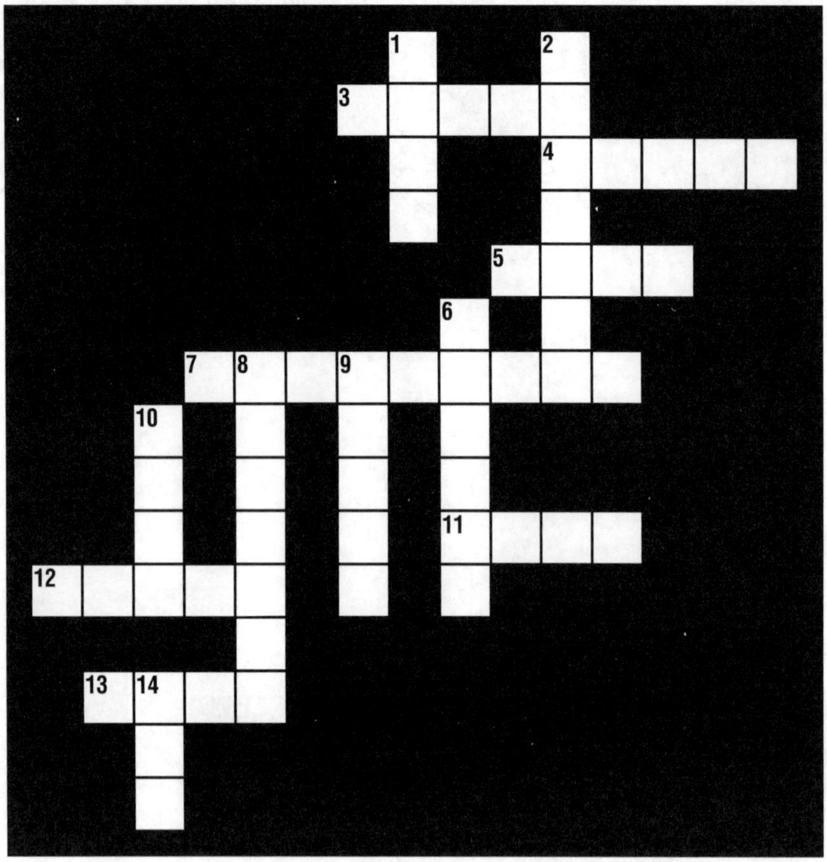

Across

3. Fruit ______ is my favorite drink.
4. A ______ is cold vegetables.
5. Steak and hamburgers are two kinds of ______.
7. I like ______ cake.
11. There's ______ milk in the refrigerator.
12. Oranges and apples are two kinds of ______.
13. How ______ oranges do you need?

Down

1. How ______ tea do you drink?
2. There's cake for ______.
6. Could I have some water, ______?
8. A ______ diet has a lot of fruit and vegetables.
9. I love cake and ice ______.
10. A ______ is a list of all the food in a restaurant.
14. We don't have ______ coffee.

B Complete the paragraph with words from the box.

vegetables	dessert	
~~have~~	ice cream	pie

On Thanksgiving Day in the United States, we (1) ___have___ a special dinner. We eat roast turkey with a lot of (2) ______________. For (3) ______________, we have pumpkin or pecan (4) ______________ and (5) ______________. It is always a very big meal; there is a lot of food!

C Write about what you eat when it is a special occasion in your country. Use words from the unit.

____

____

____

____

HEALTH

UNIT 10

Lesson A GRAMMAR AND VOCABULARY

A Label the body parts.

hand knee head foot ear stomach
arm back leg face finger chest

1. ____________ 7. ____________
2. ____________ 8. ____________
3. ____________ 9. ____________
4. ____________ 10. ____________
5. ____________ 11. ____________
6. ____________ 12. ____________

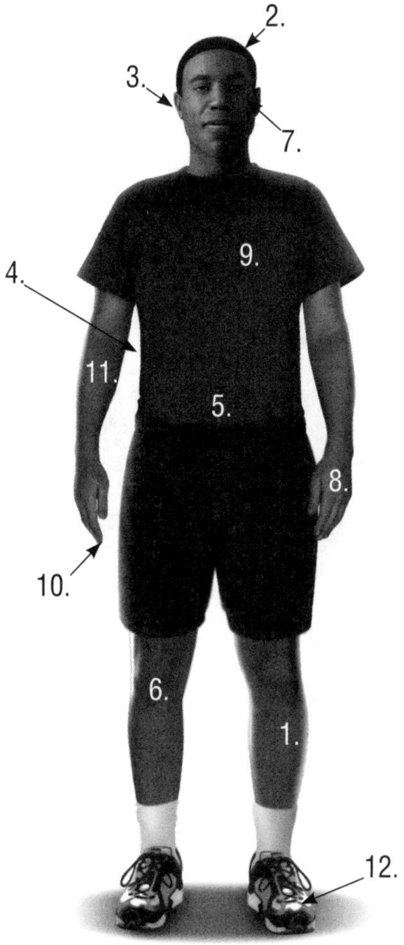

B Write the adjective in the correct box.

well terrible OK sick great

☺	☹

C Write the name of the problem.

1. My chest hurts. I have a cough.
2. My head hurts. I have a ____________.
3. I feel very hot. I have a ____________.
4. My stomach hurts. I have a ____________.
5. My back hurts. I have a ____________.

D Answer the questions.

1. How do you feel today? ____________
2. How does your friend feel today? ____________
3. How does your teacher look today? ____________
4. Does your friend look tired today? ____________

Lesson B GRAMMAR AND VOCABULARY

A Label the health problems.

cold backache toothache sore throat headache

1. ______________

2. ______________

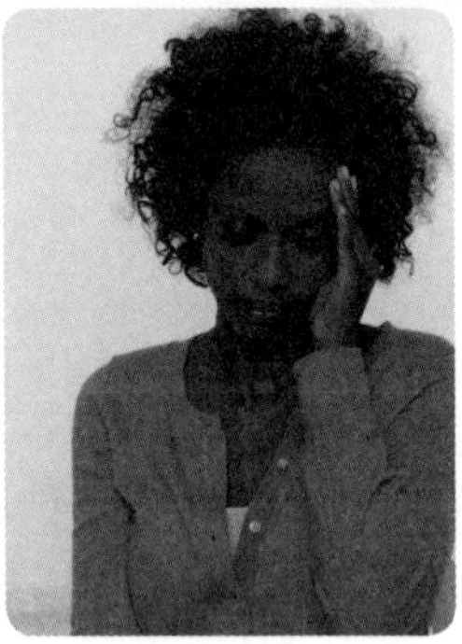

3. ______________

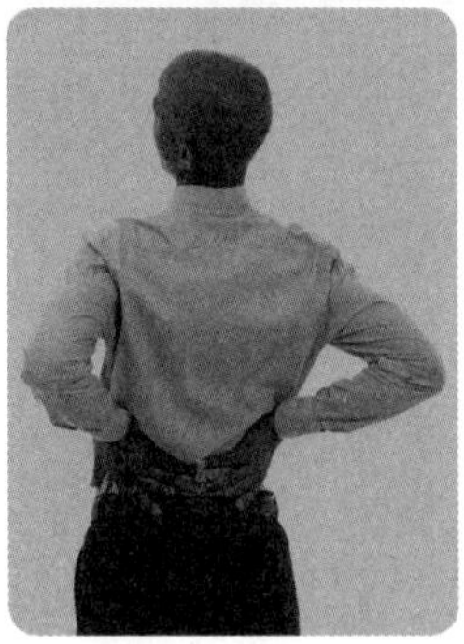

4. ______________

5. ______________

B Read the descriptions. Then write the health problems from exercise **A.**

1. John plays football. He doesn't feel good. His back hurts terribly.

   He has ______________________________.

2. Elena doesn't feel good. She has a cough and a sore throat. She has a fever, and she feels very tired all day.

   She has ______________________________.

3. Marcus can't talk. He can eat ice cream and fruit, but he can't eat hot food because it hurts a lot.

   He has ______________________________.

4. Annie is going to the dentist now. Her tooth hurts a lot. She takes some pain reliever, but it doesn't help.

   She has ______________________________.

5. Lynn works on the computer all day. She has sore eyes and her head hurts.

   She has ______________________________.

C Read the conversation out loud. Underline the stressed syllables of the important words.

Doctor: How are you today?

Patient: I have a terrible stomachache.

Doctor: Where does it hurt?

Patient: Right here.

Doctor: I need to examine you.

Lesson C GRAMMAR AND VOCABULARY

A Write the correct verb from the box. You can use some verbs more than once.

see go lie take

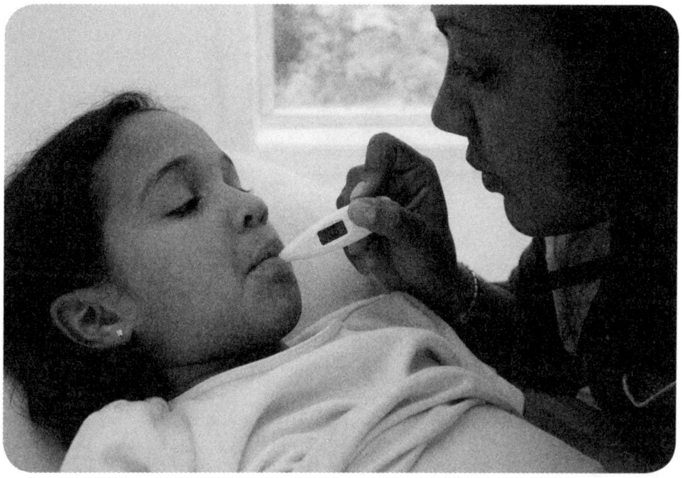

1. __________ to bed
2. __________ a doctor
3. __________ some pain reliever
4. __________ down
5. __________ cough medicine
6. __________ a dentist

B Write advice for these problems. Use your own ideas with *should* or *shouldn't.*

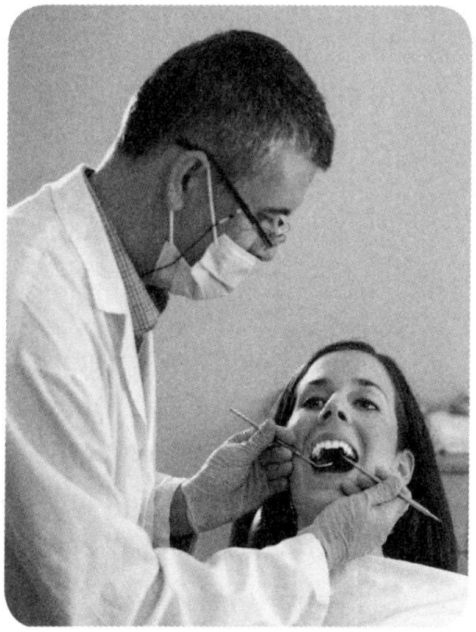

1. Your friend says, "I have a toothache."
   Advice: You __________
2. Your friend says, "I have a sore throat."
   Advice: __________
3. Your friend says, "My knee hurts."
   Advice: __________
4. Your friend says, "I have a backache."
   Advice: __________
5. Your friend says, "I feel very tired."
   Advice: __________

C Unscramble the sentences in the conversation.

Young-Mi: I have a fever and a headache. (should / do / what / I) __________ ?

Susan: (go / you / home / should) __________ .

Young-Mi: (go / should / to / I / English / class) __________ ?

Susan: (you / no / shouldn't) __________ .

(you / to / bed / go / should) __________ .

Lesson D READING AND WRITING

A Read the article.

What You Should Know About the Flu

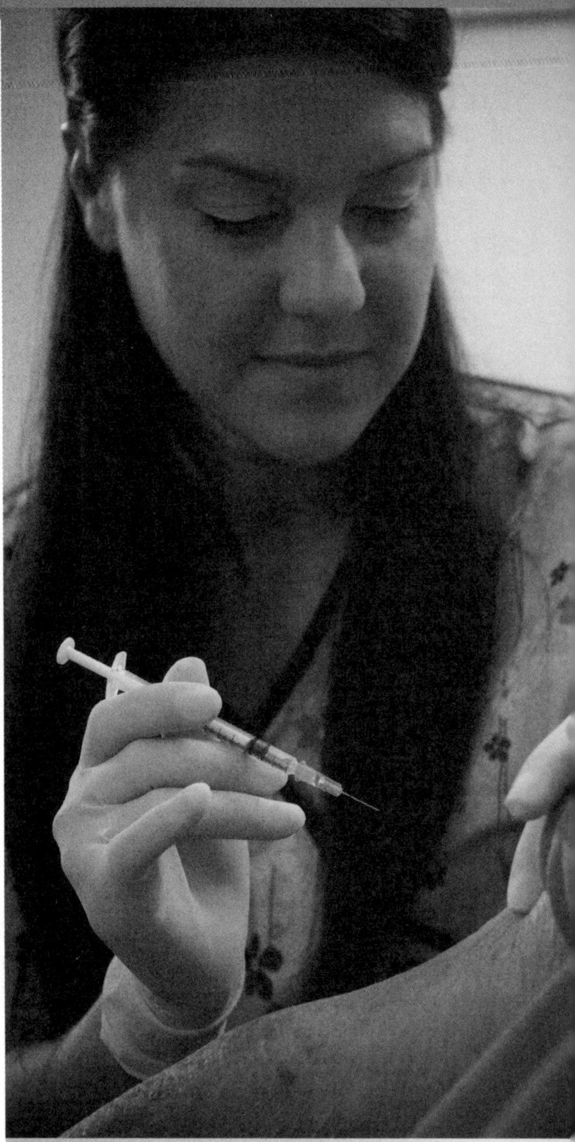

Many people are very afraid of influenza, or flu, but there are many different kinds of flu. They are different every year. Some are terrible, and others are not very bad. Some kinds can go from animals to people. And some kinds of influenza kill many people—50 million people from 1918 to 1920!

There are some easy things you can do to prevent flu.

- You should always cover your mouth when you cough.
- You should wash your hands many times every day. You shouldn't touch your face.
- A cough is a symptom of the flu. People with a bad cough shouldn't go to work or to school. They should stay home. They should call a doctor if they feel very sick.

You should do these things to stay safe during a time of flu.

B Circle **T** for *true* or **F** for *false*.

1. There are two kinds of flu.	T	F
2. The flu is the same every year.	T	F
3. The flu was very bad in 1918.	T	F
4. Washing your hands can prevent the flu.	T	F
5. Touching your face can prevent the flu.	T	F
6. People with the flu should stay home.	T	F

C Write four things you can do to prevent a toothache.

To prevent a toothache, you should brush your teeth three times a day.

____

____

____

D Complete the paragraph with *should* or *shouldn't*.

Here are some remedies for a headache. You ______________ take pain reliever. You ______________ listen to music, and you ______________ watch TV. You ______________ go to bed and sleep. If the headache doesn't stop, you ______________ go to the doctor.

E Write about remedies for a different health problem.

____

____

____

____

____

____

____

Review

Solve the crossword puzzle with vocabulary and grammar from this unit.

Across

1. a short word for "influenza"
2. You have ten ______ on your hands.
4. She has a ______ throat. It hurts a lot.
6. Doctors look at their patients. They ______ them.
7. You have a cough. You ______ take cough medicine.
8. I have a headache. My head ______.
9. What's the ______ with her?
10. You have a cold. You ______ go to school.

Down

1. I feel very hot. I have a ______.
2. I ______ tired.
3. My stomach doesn't feel good. I have a ______.
5. I feel very, very good. I feel ______.
6. You have two ______ on your head.
7. a sign that you are sick

MAKING PLANS

Lesson A GRAMMAR AND VOCABULARY

A Match the correct sentence with each picture.

a. We go out for dinner every Friday.
b. I have a party on my birthday.
c. I go to the movies with my friends.
d. We go to a game every Sunday.
e. We have a barbecue every summer.
f. We have a family meal on Sunday.

1. ____________________

2. ____________________

3. ____________________

4. ____________________

5. ____________________

6. ____________________

B Write questions and answers with *be going to* about people's weekend plans.

	Daniel	Mary	Mr. and Mrs. Kim	you
have a family meal	no	yes	yes	
travel	yes	no	yes	
go to the movies	yes	no	no	

1. What is Daniel going to do this weekend? He isn't going to have a family meal. He's going to ____________________. He's ____________________.

2. (Mary) ____________________

____

____

3. (Mr. and Mrs. Kim) ____________________

____

____

4. (you) ____________________

____

____

Lesson B GRAMMAR AND VOCABULARY

A Read the article and write about Marit's holiday plans.

> My name is Lars. I'm from Oslo, in Norway. We have lots of holidays.
>
> Norway's Independence Day is May 17. It's our national holiday. I'm going to wear Norwegian clothes. We always sing Norwegian songs and walk around the city with Norwegian flags.
>
> *Jonsok* is a Norwegian summer holiday. It's on June 23. We usually make a big fire and sing all night. I'm not going to go to bed!
>
> Christmas is a Norwegian winter holiday. It's on December 25. We like to have a big family meal. We're going to make special cookies and cakes. And I give presents to my family and friends.

1. On May 17, he's going to wear Norwegian clothes.
2. He's going to ______
3. He ______
4. On June 23, ______
5. ______
6. ______
7. On December 25, ______
8. ______
9. ______

B Write information about three holidays in your country.

Holiday	Plans
a. a national holiday name: ______ date: ______	I'm going to ______ ______ We're going to ______ ______
b. a summer holiday name: ______ date: ______	______ ______ ______ ______
c. a winter holiday name: ______ date: ______	______ ______ ______ ______

Lesson C GRAMMAR AND VOCABULARY

A Write the profession.

1. He would like to be an actor, so he's going to study acting ______________.
2. They would like to be doctors, so they're going to study ______________.
3. She would like to be a lawyer, so she's going to study ______________.
4. He would like to be a teacher, so he's going to study ______________.
5. She would like to be a musician, so she's going to study ______________.
6. We would like to be software engineers, so we're going to study ______________.

B Complete the conversation. Use *would like to.*

Angie: What's the matter?

Matt: I don't like my work! I (get) would like to get ______________ a new job.

Angie: Well, (what, do) ______________?

Matt: I don't know.

Angie: (you, work) ______________ in an office?

Matt: No, I ______________. Offices are boring.

Angie: Well, what about in a school? (you, be) ______________ a teacher?

Matt: No, I ______________. I don't like children.

Angie: Hmmm . . . (where, work) ______________.

Matt: I'd like to work in a beautiful place outside.

Angie: Hmm . . . (you, work) ______________ in a park?

Matt: Yes, I ______________! That's a great idea.

C Answer the questions. Use *would like to* and your ideas.

1. What would you like to do this weekend?

____

2. What would you like to do next vacation?

____

3. What would you like to do next time in English class?

____

4. What would you like to do next year?

____

We asked students: What are your wishes and plans?

A Read about these people's dream jobs. Write their dream jobs from the box. One job is extra.

software engineer piano teacher
doctor banker actor

Jeff: "I would like to help sick people. I need to study a lot. In the future, I would like to work in a hospital in Africa."

Job: ____________________

Cristina: "I would like to work with children. I love music—I can play the piano and the guitar, and I can sing. I would like to study in Europe. In the future, I would like to work in a school."

Job: ____________________

Andres: "I love movies. I'm going to make movies with my friends—we're going to use a computer and a video camera. Then I'm going to save money and go to Hollywood. I would like to get a job there."

Job: ____________________

Grace: "I think computers are very interesting. I would like to come up with ways for people to use them better. I am going to study in Australia next year. I would like to get a job in the capital of my country."

Job: ____________________

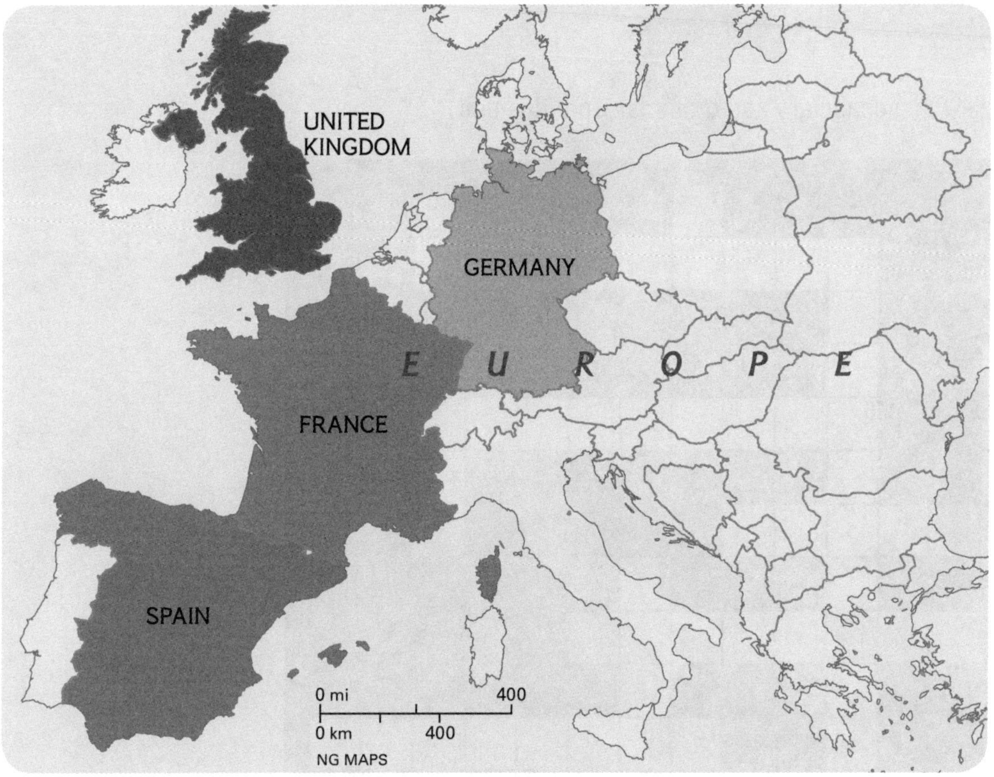

B Write the paragraph again. Use capital letters and punctuation.

i would like to travel in europe i want to visit france, england, spain, and germany i need a lot of money i'm going to get a weekend job and i'm going to work every saturday and every sunday i'm going to save all my money then i'm going to make plans for my trip i would like to go to europe next summer.

C Write about your wishes and plans for the future.

UNIT 11

Review

A Solve the crossword puzzle with vocabulary and grammar from this unit.

Across

2. I ______ have a party. It's my plan. (3 words)
6. Susan ______ study nursing. It's her plan. (3 words)
8. I ______ be a teacher. It's my goal. (3 words)
10. Ruth plays the piano. She's a ______.
12. Nicolas studied ______. Now he's a doctor.
13. special day

Down

1. I would like to ______ to a game.
2. Mike and Janie got married ten years ago. It's their ______.
3. "Would you like to be a doctor?" "No, I ______."
4. breakfast, lunch, or dinner
5. Lisa studied law. Now she's a ______.
7. We're going to go ______ for dinner at a Chinese restaurant.
9. We're going to ______ a barbecue.
11. I go to ______ movies every weekend.

B Complete the conversation with words from the box.

party	are going to
~~would like~~	is going to
family	

For my graduation, I (1) ___would like___ to have a (2) ______________ meal. My mom (3) ______________ make *memelas,* and my aunts, uncles, and cousins (4) ______________ to come. I would like to have a (5)______________ with my friends, too!

ON THE MOVE

UNIT 12

Lesson A GRAMMAR AND VOCABULARY

A Complete the sentences with verbs from the box.

return arrive go come move leave stay

1. Every morning, I __________ my house at eight o'clock, and I get on the bus.
2. I __________ at school at eight forty-five.
3. I don't __________ home for lunch. I __________ at school, and I eat lunch in the cafeteria.
4. In the afternoon, I __________ home at four thirty.
5. We're Japanese. We __________ from Tokyo.
6. Every summer we __________ to our beach house on Kyushu Island.

B Write the simple past tense of the verb.

	Simple past tense		Simple past tense
1. live		**5.** move	
2. go		**6.** stay	
3. arrive		**7.** return	
4. come		**8.** leave	

C Ameena is an international student. Write sentences about her life using the simple past tense.

1. live (Australia / ~~New Zealand~~)
   She lived in Australia. She didn't live in New Zealand.
2. go to (Melbourne / ~~Sydney~~)
   ____
3. move to (Canberra / ~~Perth~~)
   ____
4. stay in (an apartment / ~~a hotel~~)
   ____
5. return to (her home country / ~~Australia~~)
   ____

D Write simple past tense questions. Use the words in parentheses.

1. I arrived late. (when) *When did you arrive?*
2. They moved to a new house. (where) __________________?
3. He left his hometown (when) __________________?
4. She lived in Europe. (how long) __________________?
5. They went to a restaurant. (when) __________________?
6. We stayed in a hotel. (where) __________________?

Lesson B GRAMMAR AND VOCABULARY

Javier in 1998

Javier now

A Write the year in words.

1. 1995 nineteen ninety-five
2. 2012 ______________________
3. 1989 ______________________
4. 2004 ______________________
5. I was born in ______________________.
6. This year is ______________________.

B Javier is a famous businessman. Read the interview. Complete the sentences with the simple past tense.

Reporter: (when you arrive) ______________________ in this country?

Javier: I (came) ______________________ here in 1998. I (not know) ______________________ any English. I (go) ______________________ to school for two years.

Reporter: (why you leave) ______________________ your country?

Javier: I (leave) ______________________ because I (not have) ______________________ a job.

Reporter: (where you live) ______________________ in 2000?

Javier: I (live) ______________________ in a very small apartment. Then I started my computer company, and I worked very hard. In 2005, I moved to a big house. My father and mother came here.

Reporter: (when you return) ______________________ to your home country?

Javier: I (not return) ______________________ for a long time. Then I (return) ______________________ there in 2013 for a visit. I (stay) ______________________ with my brother for a month. I was so happy!

Lesson C GRAMMAR AND VOCABULARY

A What do people do when they move? Write the verb.

sell stop buy pack have get close sell

1. ______________ a farewell party

2. ______________ their house

3. ______________ the tickets

4. ______________ their bags

5. ______________ a passport

6. ______________ the bank account

7. ______________ their car

8. ______________ their mail

B Look at Ed's list. Write questions and answers with the simple past tense.

Things to do
1. study for the English test ✓
2. get money from the bank ✓
3. go to the supermarket
4. call David ✓
5. check e-mail

1. Did he study for the English test? Yes, he did.
2. ______________________________?
   ______________________________.
3. ______________________________?
   ______________________________.
4. ______________________________?
   ______________________________.
5. ______________________________?
   ______________________________.

C What did you do yesterday? Write five things.

1. I ______________________________.
2. I ______________________________.
3. I ______________________________.
4. ______________________________.
5. ______________________________.

Lesson D READING AND WRITING

A Read the e-mail.

From: cperez@gomail.com
To: andy95@gomail.com
Subject: The Trip!!

Hey Andy,

We had a great time on our trip! We left home on April 1. We arrived in New York in the morning, and we visited Times Square and the famous stores. The next day, we stayed in New York, and we went to a very big museum.

On April 3, we went to Washington, D.C. We saw many interesting places, like the White House. The next day, we went shopping. I was very tired.

On April 5, we left Washington, D.C., and went to Miami. Our hotel was at the beach, and the weather was warm and beautiful. We went swimming and bought presents. I bought a present for you, too!

We left the United States on April 7 and returned home. It was a great trip.

See you soon!
Chris

A Answer the questions.

1. Did Chris like his trip?

   ______________________________________.

2. When did Chris start his trip?

   ______________________________________.

3. Where did he go first?

   ______________________________________.

4. How long did he stay in Washington, D.C.?

   ______________________________________.

5. What did he buy in Miami?

   ______________________________________.

B Complete the brochure.

Great American Cities

April 1 Leave home. Arrive in ____________. Go to Times Square, the Statue of Liberty, and many famous ____________.

April 2 A day at the Metropolitan Museum of Art.

April 3 Leave New York in the morning. Arrive in ____________. Go on a tour of the ____________ House, the Capitol, and the Smithsonian Museums.

April 4 Free time to go ____________.

April 5 Go to ____________. Stay in a hotel on the ____________.

April 6 Go swimming and buy ____________ for your friends.

April 7 Leave the United States. Arrive home.

C Write an e-mail about a trip. Use the simple past tense. It can be a real trip or an imaginary trip.

____

____

____

____

____

____

____

Review

A Solve the crossword puzzle with vocabulary and grammar from this unit.

Across

2. simple past tense of *come*
3. simple past tense of *have*
8. He ______ from England to Australia last year.
10. 1990 in words
11. simple past tense of *buy*
12. simple past tense of *leave*
13. When ______ arrive in this country? (2 words)
14. simple past tense of *stay*

Down

1. You need a ______ to go to another country.
4. I have a bank ______.
5. At a ______ party, you say goodbye.
6. simple past tense of *arrive*
7. simple past tense of *go*
9. I lived in Japan. I (not) ______ in Korea. (2 words)

B Complete the paragraph with words from the box.

going-away
got ~~moved~~
tickets packed
sold car

When we (1) ___moved___ to Canada last year, we (2) ______________ our apartment and our (3) ______________. We did a lot of things before we moved. We (4) ______________ a lot of things, (5) ______________ our passports, and bought (6) ______________. Our friends had a (7) ______________ party for us—that was the best thing!